A Bit of Everything

Für Otto

Acknowledgments

I would like to thank all the following people for helping me make this dream possible.

First, my wife, for supporting me and putting up with all the mess I make when I cook and for always cleaning up regardless of how many pots and pans, I use. Being a great taster for all the dishes I make, both good and bad. And for giving me the confidence to believe in myself.

My son, Otto, for being a huge inspiration for writing this book.

My dad, sister, and especially my mum for proofreading the booking and helping me develop the dishes.

My very large extended family for providing inspiration and lots of food filled fun days at all the family gatherings.

Finally, the American Publishers Inc for working with me to turn my dream into reality.

Table of Contents

INTRO 7

WHY I AM WRITING THIS BOOK 8

LOSING WEIGHT AND GETTING FITTER 9

    PASTA 11

    GERMAN CUISINE 38

MY MOTHER'S INFLUENCE 40

    MEAT 50

MY EXPERIENCE WITH MEAT 52

MEAT TEMPERATURE CHART 53

    DIFFERENT CUTS OF MEAT 54

FILLET 55

SIRLOIN 56

RIBEYE 57

RUMP 58

TOPSIDE / SILVERSIDE 58

SHIN 59

BRISKET 59

    FISH 85

    POULTRY 96

STAPLES 97

MY BROTHER 128

    POTATO 130

VERSATILITY 131

    SLOW COOKING 148

EASY COOKING 149

    DESSERTS 160

SWEET TOOTH 161

    BABY FOOD IDEAS 184

DISCOVERY 186

ABOUT THE AUTHOR 209

Intro

Most people writing a cookbook will say that they started loving food when they were young and that they have always been passionate about cooking and food. For me, however, this was not the case.

When I was younger, I was an incredibly fussy eater, and there was a very small list of foods that I would eat. I think, for around 6-7 years, I ate the same plain ham sandwich on brown bread for lunch every day at school. My mum would occasionally mix it up, putting in leftover spaghetti with a bit of ketchup, but that was the extent of my packed lunches.

On the odd occasion when we would go out to a restaurant to eat when visiting my grandparents in Germany, I would order plain spaghetti with a bit of butter.

I distinctly remember one birthday meal, I asked for a king-size chicken and mushroom pot noodle with a slice of bread to put the noodles on.

I used to bake with my mum every now and again, but it was few and far between.

When I was 20, I moved out of my parents' house and into a flat with a friend. He was very into his cooking and tried new and exciting dishes with interesting flavours. It was at this point that I started working as a butcher in a local farm shop. One of the other butchers was a very keen cook who gave me lots of ideas on what to cook. With prime access to all the different cuts of meat, I had the opportunity to research different things to try. I also had the opportunity to talk to the chefs and a few of the regular customers to get ideas from.

This is when I started to really enjoy cooking and started getting better at it. This came in very handy, impressing my new girlfriend (my now wife) with my cooking ability. I also started to come up with my own recipes from the different dishes that I had cooked. The first dish that I remember cooking for her was a rack of lamb with steamed kale and Pommes Anna.

All the recipes in this book are ones that I have created myself by experimenting with different flavours and techniques, or ones that I have adapted to make my own. For example, I wasn't sure what to call the dauphinoise potatoes recipe, so I picked the recipe that had the closest similarity to my recipe.

Why I Am Writing This Book

No, I am not a chef, and no, I am not an influencer who makes videos about cooking. I am just a man who has dedicated a lot of time and effort to cooking good food for my family.

In mine and my wife's family, there are great cooks who make some amazing food. My wife's great-grandmother died a couple of years ago, and the whole family kept saying how nice her mashed potatoes were, and how the recipe had died with her as it wasn't written down anywhere. This is one of the reasons that I am writing this book—to preserve all the great family recipes for the future generations of our family that we have access to.

I am also writing this for my son, Otto, so that he can cook all the recipes that he will eat growing up and potentially feed his kids in the future. Being able to cook lots of different types of dishes and lots of different types of ingredients is a great life skill to have and has done me a lot of good.

Being half German and half English, there are some similarities between the two different cuisines, but there are some major differences. There are some foods that you can only get in Germany and, likewise, in England. I live in England now, but I go back to Germany a couple of times a year so that I can see my family. Every time I go back to Germany, there are a few different dishes that I eat without fail, as they are impossible to get in England. I have tried my best to recreate them while at home so I can bring the taste of Germany back to England.

Being half German is very important to me; I am very proud of it, and I want my son to be as well. Teaching him all about his family and the food that I ate while growing up is very important to me as well.

The only food that Germany is famous for is lots of sausages, sauerkraut, and beer. These are stereotypes for a reason, as they are eaten a lot in Germany, but there are also so many dishes that are not widely known in England, which is a shame, as they are some of the best dishes I have ever eaten.

Losing Weight and Getting Fitter

Just after my son was born in December of 2024, I realised that my slow weight gain had gone too far and that I had reached a point where I was no longer happy with how I looked. After I finished my paternity leave, I decided to take weight loss seriously, as I wanted to be able to do active stuff with my son without getting out of breath running up the stairs to get something.

I also realised that if I carried on gaining weight the way I was, I would start to damage my body, and by looking after myself now, I was going to help myself live longer and be able to do all the active things that my dad did with me growing up, with my son.

I have signed myself up to do the 3 Peaks Challenge at the end of June of this year to help raise money for the Huntington's Disease Association. It is something that I have always wanted to do and something that I would have to train for, which would help me lose weight. I also will have three of my best friends (who are crazy enough to do it) with me without any persuading. If you don't know, the 3 Peaks Challenge is walking up the three tallest peaks in the UK within 24 hours. It starts at Ben Nevis, which is the tallest mountain in Scotland. From there, you go down to Scafell Pike, which is the tallest Mountain in England, and then finish at Snowdon, which is the tallest mountain in Wales. I have included a QR code that will take you straight to the JustGiving page if you would like to donate. They are a brilliant charity that helps people suffering from Huntington's Disease and their families.

I started running again for a number of reasons:

1) I am too cheap to pay for a gym membership.
2) I need to walk the dogs in the morning anyway, so it wasn't taking away any time I could be spending with my son after work.
3) I am getting myself fitter, which I will need to do in order to complete the 3 Peaks Challenge.

After doing more research into weight loss, I quickly realised that if I am in a caloric deficit, I will be slowly losing weight. I, along with lots of other people, assumed that it takes a crazy diet or only eating plain chicken and rice to lose weight. It was only when I got a calorie tracking app that I realised how much my little evening snacks were and how big my portions really were.

The main thing I have done to lose weight was to stop the unhealthy evening snacking. I figured out that I was snacking, not because I was hungry, but just for something to do while watching TV. Along with cutting the snacking, I have started cutting down my portion sizes, and doing this made me realise that I was eating way more than I needed to be full. While counting my calories, I realised that I was still able to eat the food I enjoyed, and it didn't have to be limited to boring salads or extremely small amounts of food. A lot of the recipes that I have included in this book are low in calories and can easily be part of the diet of someone who is looking to lose weight.

It is very important to have a balanced and healthy diet, especially when you are trying to lose weight. Making sure that you hit all the major food groups helps keep you fuller, eating a smaller quantity of food. I like to try and add beans and proteins to meals where I can, which helps build up the fibre and nutrients in my diet.

When I first started dieting and calorie counting, I had to weigh my food, so I knew how much I needed to input into my app. It was when I started doing this that I realised how big my portions had been.

Cutting down portion sizes can work for some people, but it is not for everyone. A way to help fill you up if you are looking to cut down on calories but stay full when you eat is to eat more of high-volume low-calorie food, such as lettuce, tomatoes, and mushrooms, and increase the amount of high protein and high fibre foods.

We completed the challenge in 23 hours and 40 minutes. It was the hardest physical thing I have ever done in my life. At the same time, I am incredibly proud of what we had achieved and the money that we raised, and I couldn't have wish for a better team to do it with, however, I will not be in a rush to do it again. It will always be something that I can look back on with a hole mix of emotions.

Homemade Pasta
FEEDS 2

Making your own pasta can seem a bit daunting, but it is much easier than it sounds. It is very basic and can be done even if you do not have a pasta maker. However, it is a lot easier if you do have a pasta maker.

 **Ingredients:**

- 100g OO flour
- 1 whole egg
- 1 egg yolk

 **Method:**

- Mix the flour and eggs in a bowl until combined.
- If the dough is a bit sticky, then add a pinch of flour at a time until you can poke it and your finger does not stick to the dough.
- Make sure not to over mix it as you don't want the pasta to be too tough. After kneading, you still want the dough to be nice and soft.
- Wrap the dough in cling film and leave to rest in the fridge for at least an hour but can be for longer. For example, you can make the dough in the morning and then use it for dinner that evening.
- Once the dough has rested, take it out of the fridge and unwrap it. you will notice that it is now sticky again. Flour the worktop and knead it for around a minute or so until it is not sticky anymore.
- If you are not using a pasta maker, then simply roll the dough out on a well-floured work surface until you have reached your desired thickness. Then loosely roll the dough to make it easier to cut.
- If you are using a pasta maker, set it to the widest setting and roll it through 1-3 times dusting each side with flour each time.
- Then go down each setting one at a time flouring both sides each time. Stop when you get to the penultimate thickness so that it is not too thin.
- Cut the pasta in half so that it is not too long and then put it through the cutting setting to turn it into tagliatelle or spaghetti.
- It is best to cook it as soon as you can after that.
- Put the pasta into boiling water and cook for around 3 minutes.

Prawn and Chorizo Orzo

FEEDS 4 WITH SIDES

This is a very versatile dish that has lots of different permutations. Lots of different ingredients can be added or taken away to change the dish, depending on what you want.

Ingredients:

- 400g orzo
- 400g tin of chopped tomatoes x2
- 2 finely diced shallots
- 100g finely diced chorizo
- 250g-350g prawns (my preference is the small ones as they are then evenly distributed)
- 30g fresh basil
- Salt and pepper
- 350ml vegetable stock
- Hard cheese such as Pecorino or Parmesan

Method:

- Place the shallots in a medium-high heat frying pan with a splash of oil and cook for 4-5 minutes until they start to become translucent.
- Remove the skin from the chorizo, finely dice it and add into the frying pan and cook for 5 minutes. Add in the prawns and cook for an additional 5 minutes.
- Add the chopped tomatoes into the pan and mix well.
- Add in the uncooked orzo and stir until it is fully incorporated.
- Add in the vegetable stock and stir until combined.
- Set the heat to low – medium and simmer until the orzo has absorbed the stock. Once it is all absorbed the orzo should be cooked. If it still needs some time, then add a bit more stock.
- Stir every couple of minutes so ensure it doesn't stick to the bottom of the pan.
- Plate up and grate the cheese on top.

Veggie Orzo

FEEDS 4 - 6

This veggie option is a great alternative, which adds different flavors and is a very refreshing dish.

Ingredients:

- 500g orzo
- 400g tin of chopped tomatoes x2
- 2 finely diced shallots
- 100g capers
- 100g sliced black olives
- Handful of fresh basil
- Salt and pepper
- Hard cheese such as Pecorino or Parmesan
- 350ml vegetable stock

Method:

- Place the shallots in a medium-high heat frying pan with a splash of oil and cook for 4-5 minutes, until they start to become translucent.
- Add the capers and olives to the frying pan. Cook for an additional 10 minutes.
- Add the uncooked orzo into the pan and mix well.
- Add the tinned tomatoes into the pan and mix well.
- Add in the vegetable stock and reduce the heat down to a simmer.
- Stir the sauce every 2-4 minutes to make sure nothing is sticking.
- Cook until all the liquid has been absorbed.
- When the liquid has been absorbed the orzo should be fully cooked, if not then add in some more stock and cook until absorbed and the orzo is cooked.
- Mix in the basil and a sprinkle of black pepper.
- Plate up and grate the cheese on top.

Spicy Chicken Pasta

FEEDS 6

This fresh and warm dish can be served all year round, as it can warm you up in the winter. Also, with the chillis, it tastes fresh and snappy, perfect for a summer meal out in the garden with the family.

Ingredients:

- 500g penne
- 2 x 400g tinned chopped tomatoes
- 2 sliced mild chillis
- 2 finely diced chicken breasts
- 200g spinach
- 3 minced cloves of garlic
- A pinch of salt
- A pinch of pepper
- Grated hard cheese (I prefer to use Pecorino Romano)

Method:

- Bring a pot of water to a rolling boil, add a heavy pinch of salt, put in the penne, and cook until done.
- Meanwhile, put a splash of oil in a frying pan on low heat, add the minced garlic, and cook for 1-2 minutes until golden brown, stirring frequently to make sure it doesn't burn.
- Add in the chillis and chicken and cook for 5 minutes until the chicken starts to cook.
- Add in the spinach and wilt it down.
- Add both tins of chopped tomatoes and stir until fully combined.
- Add salt and pepper to taste and reduce.
- Once the pasta is cooked and add a good splash of pasta water. Strain the pasta before adding it to the sauce and mix until fully incorporated.
- Plate it up and top with the cheese of your choice.

Seafood Spaghetti

FEEDS 4-6

This dish is perfect for the summer. It's how I learned how to make my own pasta sauce.

Ingredients:

- 500g spaghetti
- 300g assorted seafood (I use prawns, deshelled muscles, and squid, but any selection of seafood can be used. This can be frozen)
- 1 400g tin of chopped tomatoes
- 2 tablespoons of tomato puree
- Salt & pepper
- Grated hard cheese such as Pecorino or Parmesan
- 1 onion or 2 shallots, finely diced
- 4 cloves of minced garlic
- Sunflower oil
- 2 tablespoons of soy sauce
- 2 tablespoons of balsamic glaze
- Chilli flakes (optional)

Method:

- Bring a saucepan of salted water to a rolling boil, add the spaghetti, and cook until al dente.
- While the spaghetti is cooking, add the onion to a large frying pan (for which you have a lid) with the oil and cook for 4-5 minutes on a medium–high heat until it starts to become translucent. Add in the garlic and cook for a further 2 minutes, stirring to prevent burning. Add the tomato puree and cook for an additional 3-5 minutes until the 'raw smell' stops.
- Add the seafood and tin of tomatoes into the frying pan. Turn the heat down to low-medium. Stir the sauce every 2-4 minutes to make sure that nothing is burning. Add the soy sauce and balsamic glaze to the sauce and stir until fully incorporated.
- Turn the heat down and 6reduce the sauce until it has reached the desired thickness. This should take 10-20 minutes.
- Strain the pasta and add it to the sauce, mixing it well until the pasta is fully incorporated into the sauce.
- Plate up with the cheese grated over the top.

Creamy Orzo

FEEDS 4

This is a very rich, creamy dish, which is a great winter warmer and works very well as a main with sides or as part of a larger sharing meal.

Ingredients:

- 400g tin of chopped tomatoes x2
- 300ml single cream
- 1 onion
- 3 minced cloves of garlic
- 250g prawns
- 500g orzo
- 1-1.5L vegetable stock
- 100g butter
- 50g grated Parmesan

Method:

- Finely dice the onion and add to a medium-heat frying pan with half of the butter and cook until it starts to soften and go translucent. This should take 5-10 minutes.
- Add the minced garlic to the frying pan and cook for an additional 5 minutes.
- Add chopped tomatoes.
- Add the prawns into the pan, along with the cream, and stir well, so that everything is combined.
- Cook for 5 – 10 minutes until all cooked and combined.
- Transfer the contents of the pan to a blender and blend on low until smooth.
- Add the orzo into the pan and cook for a couple of minutes until it starts to go light brown.
- Add the sauce back into the pan along with 400ml of vegetable stock and cook on low.
- Cook until the liquid has been absorbed and repeat until the orzo is cooked. This should take 3-5 times but keep tasting to make sure that the orzo does not get overcooked.
- Once the orzo is cooked to the desired texture, take it off the heat. Add in the second half of the butter and the grated Parmesan and stir well so that they are fully incorporated.

Creamy Mushroom Linguine

FEEDS 4

This is a great dish that can work all year round, but personally, I think this dish works best in the autumn, just when the weather starts to turn and get colder.

Ingredients:

- 150g shiitake mushrooms (works with other mushrooms if shiitake are not available)
- 1 white onion
- 4 cloves of garlic
- 200ml double cream
- 200g cherry tomatoes
- 360g – 500g dried linguine roughly 90g per person
- Salt and black pepper
- 1tbsp of tomato puree
- Grated Parmesan/Pecorino Romano

Method:

- Finely dice the onion and put in a large frying pan with a dash of oil on medium heat and cook for 5-10 minutes until translucent. Then add in the minced garlic, tomato puree, salt, and black pepper.
- Cook for a further 5 minutes and add in the quartered cherry tomatoes.
- Put a lid on the frying pan, reduce the heat, and let everything simmer for 10 minutes until the tomatoes have started to break down. Stir every couple of minutes to prevent sticking.
- Place the pasta in a pan of boiling water and cook until done.
- Roughly chop the shiitake mushrooms and add into the frying pan. Replace the lid and let it cook until the mushrooms have reached the desired consistency. (For me, this takes around 10 minutes.)
- Add the cream and mix well so that it's fully incorporated, and let it simmer for 5 minutes.
- Once the pasta is cooked, add a good splash of pasta water into the sauce and mix well. Drain the pasta, add it to the pan with the sauce, and mix it all together well.
- Plate up and top with the grated cheese.

Creamy Chicken Linguine

FEEDS 4

This dish differs slightly from the one on page 27 due to the chicken giving it a different flavour profile and the spinach adding another texture. This can very easily be made vegetarian by substituting the chicken for tofu.

Ingredients:

- 500g diced chicken (thighs/breasts)
- 1 white onion
- 4 cloves of garlic
- 200ml double cream
- 200g spinach
- 200g cherry tomatoes
- 360g – 500g dried linguine roughly 90g per person
- Salt and black pepper
- 1tbsp of tomato puree
- Grated Parmesan/Pecorino Romano
- 1tsp paprika

Method:

- Dice the chicken and put in a frying pan on medium heat with a splash of oil and cook for 5 minutes until the outside is cooked.
- Finely dice the onion and put in a frying pan on medium heat and cook for 5-10 minutes until translucent, and then add in the minced garlic, tomato puree, salt, black pepper, and spinach.
- Cook for a further 5 minutes and add in the quartered cherry tomatoes. Put a lid on the frying pan, reduce the heat, and let everything simmer for 10 minutes until the tomatoes have started to break down, stirring every couple of minutes to prevent sticking.
- Place the pasta in a pan of boiling water and cook until done.
- Add the cream and paprika and mix well so that it's fully incorporated, and let it simmer for 5 minutes.
- Once the pasta is cooked, add a good splash of pasta water into the sauce and mix in well. Drain the pasta and add it to the pan with the sauce, and mix it all together well.
- Plate up and top with the grated cheese.

Not so Traditional Carbonara

FEEDS 4

Carbonara is a very traditional Italian dish, which I have very slightly changed. I have added lime juice and zest as I love tangy flavours. To make this dish more traditional, take out the lime and swap the bacon for guanciale. Guanciale is a better ingredient to use, but I have found that it is harder and more expensive to get in the shop.

Ingredients:

- 260g dried Tagliatelle
- 4 egg yolks
- 1 egg white
- 50g Parmesan
- Bacon lardons
- Salt and black pepper
- Zest of one lime
- Juice of half a lime

Method:

- Bring a pot of water to a rolling boil and start cooking the pasta.
- Place the bacon lardons in the frying pan and cook for 10 minutes, stirring every few minutes to avoid burning. This should allow the bacon to become crispy and the fat to render out of it.
- Once the bacon is cooked, take it out of the pan and transfer the fat into a separate bowl. Mix in the egg yolks, one egg white, the Parmesan, and lime zest and juice.
- Once the pasta is cooked, put a ladle of the pasta water into the bowl and make sure that it is mixed thoroughly.
- Put the cooked pasta back into the frying pan with the heat off, and pour in the egg mixture and bacon.
- Immediately mix thoroughly to make sure that the eggs do not cook. As you start stirring the mixture in, you will start to see it turning cream

Tag Bol

FEEDS 4

After completing my first Italian cooking course I learned that spaghetti is not the correct type of pasta for this type of sauce as it just slides off. You need a wider pasta shape like tagliatelle, which the sauce can stick to.

Ingredients:

- 2 large carrots/3 medium carrots
- 3 sticks of celery
- 1 white onion
- 3 tbsp butter
- 4 cloves of garlic, minced
- 500g beef mince
- 1 beef stock cube (I like to use a stock pot)
- 200ml red wine
- 400g tinned tomatoes x2
- 360g dried tagliatelle (most pasta works if you would like something different)

Method:

- Peel and finely dice the carrots, celery, and onion, along with butter, and put in a large frying pan on a low heat. Place a lid on the frying pan, stirring every couple of minutes to make sure everything is cooking evenly.
- Cook for 5 minutes, and then add in the minced garlic and then cook for an additional 15 minutes.
- Add in the mince and break it up so that it's in small pieces.
- Add the salt and pepper and red wine. Leave the lid off and cook until the liquid has been absorbed.
- Add the tinned chopped tomatoes.
- Add the bolognese sauce and use 300ml of water to get the last of the sauce out of the jar.
- Add the stock cube and mix everything together well, and start cooking the pasta.
- Leave the lid on the frying pan until the stock cube has fully dissolved, and then take the lid off and reduce the liquid until the sauce has thickened. The sauce should be thick, and the pasta should be done around the same time. Add a splash of the pasta water into the sauce and mix well.
- Plate up the pasta and sauce and top with your cheese of choice.

Beef Ragu

Now, I know that a Spag Bol is good and easy for a midweek meal, but if you have the time to upgrade this to a ragu, then this is the way I do it. You will need a slow cooker for this recipe.

Ingredients for 6 Portions:

- 500g pasta
- 500g beef (I prefer a fattier cut like chuck, but lean also works well)
- 3tbsp tomato puree
- 2 beef stock cubes
- 700ml water
- 2 large carrots
- 3 sticks of celery
- 400g tin of chopped tomatoes
- Salt and black pepper
- 200ml red wine

Method:

- In a slow cooker, put the diced beef, roughly chopped carrots, roughly chopped celery, tomato puree, water, red wine, and beef stock cubes. Season with salt and pepper and stir well. Put the slow cooker on high for 5 hours or on low for 8 hours, depending on how much time you have. Stir every hour or so to make sure that everything is mixed well.
- Once the beef easily falls apart, pick out all the pieces and, on a separate plate, shred them.
- Put the rest of the contents of the slow cooker in a blender and blend on the slowest speed for 30 seconds–1 minute. It is done when the pieces of celery and carrot are the size of chocolate chips.
- Place this mixture into a large high-sided frying pan or saucepan and place on medium heat so that it is gently bubbling, and the sauce starts to reduce. Add the shredded beef back into the sauce and stir well so that it is evenly distributed.
- As the sauce is reducing, start cooking your pasta.
- Season the sauce to taste with salt and pepper. Once it has reached the desired consistency, I like to add the pasta to the sauce and stir it all together so that there is an even coating of sauce on the pasta. My wife, however, likes the sauce on top of the pasta, so whatever works best for you.

Creamy Tomato and Pepper Tagliatelle

FEEDS 4

This is my take on a classic dish with classic flavors.

Ingredients:

- 2 Romano peppers
- 30-40 cherry tomatoes
- 1 bulb of garlic
- 260g dried tagliatelle
- 100ml single cream
- 25g – 50g grated Pecorino Romano cheese
- Salt and pepper

Method:

- Preheat the oven to 220 °C

- In a large oven dish, put all the tomatoes cut in half, de-seed the peppers and cut into quarters, peel all the cloves of garlic and add into the dish. Drizzle oil over everything and mix well, place in the preheated oven.

- Roast for 20 - 30 minutes until its well cooked but before it gets burnt.

- Once cooked, take it out of the oven and put the contents of the dish into a blender along with the cream and cheese. Blend on low until the sauce is smooth.

- Pour the sauce into a frying pan and turn the heat on low. Add a sprinkle of salt and a heavy crack of black pepper.

- Start cooking the tagliatelle.

- Start reducing the sauce until it starts to thicken.

- Once the pasta is cooked, add a splash of the pasta water into the sauce and stir it well. Drain the pasta and add it to the sauce. Mix it well and then serve.

German Cuisine

My Mother's Influence

My mother has had a massive influence on me in a culinary sense. From when I was a young kid, she would always cook for us. She was the first person to introduce me to cooking and baking.

For every party that either my sister or I attended when we were kids, my mum would make a rainbow jelly. This was made by pouring a layer of one colour jelly into the bottom of a large clear bowl. Waiting until it sets and then pouring in a different colour on top very carefully so that the layers don't mix. This is carried on colour by colour until the whole bowl is full of different colours.

Along with the jelly, she would also always make my birthday cake. The most memorable of which was quite some years ago, when I was very healthy and wanted a healthy birthday cake. So, she took this request and found a cheesecake that used avocado as its main ingredient. The author insisted that the avocado was not the overwhelming flavour. However, whether it was the fact that it was the first time my mum had made it, or if it was that the author could not taste avocado, the cake was inedible. My father, who normally tries to find the good part of everything that my mum cooks, was not able to finish his slice. We all agreed that it was one of the worst things that she had ever cooked.

At my grandparents' house in Germany, there is a plum tree. It is a type of plum that in German is called Mirabelle. They are small yellow plums. Every year when we go over in the summer, we pick all the plums from the tree and turn them into jam. Whenever I make jam, I think of making jam with my gran mum and sister. Everyone gets involved with the process and contributes to the effort. I start by climbing the tree and picking all the plums and dropping them down to my mum, who is standing on the ground. With each full bowl, this gets taken up to my gran and sister, who are removing the stones and washing them. Once they have all been picked, my mum and I join them in the kitchen. As they continue their job, Mum and I start the cooking process and then put the finished jam into jars and let them cool before sealing and packing them away. We normally make enough jam in a day to last my grandparents for the rest of the year. This is a tradition that I look forward to passing on to my son when we go over to Germany every year.

When I'm back in Germany, the main cooked meal we eat is lunch, while the evening meal usually consists of slices of bread with meats, cheeses, and additional items, which normally include gherkins, tomato spreads, and occasionally some sushi. Growing up, I was a very fussy eater and would roll a pickled baby corn (Mais kölbchen in German) in a slice of kinder würst, which is a slice of ham that looks like a teddy bear. That was about all I would eat, with the occasional slice of bread.

German Potato Salad

FEEDS 5 AS A SIDE DISH

This versatile dish can be served either hot or cold, as the side dish of a larger meal or potentially as your contribution in a bring and share meal with friends or family.

Ingredients:

- 750g new potatoes
- 1 packet of smoked streaky bacon, typically 14 rashers
- 1 red onion
- 3tsp of smooth English mustard
- Large slash of red wine vinegar
- 20g of chives
- 30g of parsley

Method:

- Cut the new potatoes into small bite-sized pieces, place them into a pot of boiling water, and let them cook for 15-20 minutes or until you can start to see the edges go fuzzy. Strain the potatoes and set them aside.

- Finely dice the onion and place it into a large frying pan with a splash of oil and cook for 5 minutes, stirring intermittently to make sure that it does not burn, until fragrant.

- Cut the streaky bacon into small pieces and add into the frying pan. Cook the bacon until it starts to get crispy. Deglaze the frying pan with the red wine vinegar and stir well.

- Add the mustard to the bacon and onion and stir well until it is fully incorporated.

- Add the potatoes into the frying pan and stir well to make sure that everything is evenly distributed.

- Lastly, cut the parsley and chives as small as you can and mix them in the frying pan until this is also evenly distributed.

Schnitzel

FEEDS 1 PER STEAK

This is a German staple that always makes me happy and reminds me of being back in Germany with my family.

Ingredients:

- 1 pork loin steak per person
- 100g breadcrumbs per steak
- 1 egg per steak
- Salt and pepper
- Oil
- 20g Parmesan per steak (optional)

Method:

- Place a sheet of cling film on the chopping board, place a pork loin on the chopping board, and then place another sheet of cling film on top of the loin steak so that the steak is sandwiched in between pieces of cling film.
- Now, beat the loin steak nice and thin until it is 5mm or less in thickness. If you have a meat mallet to hand, then that is the best thing to use; however, the steak can easily be flattened by using other implements, such as a frying pan or saucepan, or anything else with a flat edge. If you are finding that the single layer of cling film is splitting, then add a second layer.
- Crack the egg(s) into a wide bowl and mix, then put the thin loin steak in the egg and make sure that the whole steak is covered. In a flat tray, put the breadcrumbs, salt, black pepper, and (optional) Parmesan and mix well and spread out evenly.
- Put the now egg-covered loin steak in the breadcrumbs and fully coat it, pressing the steak down to make sure the breadcrumbs are compact.
- Preheat a frying pan to a medium-high heat and put a very heavy splash of oil in the frying pan so that it just covers the bottom of the pan. Place the breaded steak in the hot frying pan and cook for 5-7 minutes on each side until golden brown and cooked through.

Käse Spätzle

FEEDS 4

This is a very authentic and traditional German recipe that always reminds me of being back in Germany. It is similar to fresh pasta but has a more dumpling-type texture. It has always been one of my favourites, and I used to love making it with my mum when I was a kid. This is usually eaten as the main alongside a side of your choice or just on its own.

Ingredients:

- 500g plain flour
- 5 eggs
- 200ml sparkling water
- 1tsp salt
- Grated cheese
- Breadcrumbs

Method:

- Put the flour and salt in a mixer and add in the eggs, mixing slowly until the eggs have been fully incorporated into the batter.
- Slowly add in the water bit at a time until the batter is smooth but not as runny as pancake batter. It should resemble a slightly thinner bread batter.
- Place this to one side and let it rest for 15-20 minutes.
- While the batter is resting, put a large pot of water onto boil with a pinch of salt.
- Preheat the oven to 180 °C.
- Once the water is boiling, put a spoon of the batter into a spätzle maker. If you do not have a spätzle maker, then a one-sided cheese grater and a spatula will work, and move the batter backwards and forwards, and the batter will slowly drop through the holes into the boiling water.
- Once that one spoonful worth of batter is in the boiling water, wait until the spätzle has risen to the top and is floating on the surface.
- Scoop the spätzle out of the water and put in an oven-safe dish. Repeat this process until all the batter has been used up.
- Grate a bit of the cheese and mix it into the spätzle. Grate the rest of the cheese on top and then add the breadcrumbs on top of that.
- Put the dish in the oven and cook for 15-25 minutes or until the cheese has melted and started to brown.
- Take the dish out of the oven, and it is ready to serve.

My Experience With Meat

For most of my life, meat has been a very big part, and I am a very big meat-eater. When I first met my wife, I was a vegan; however, this did not last very long. I think I lasted around 12-18 months. Prior to and post this, I was/am a meat lover. When I was in my early 20s, I got a job in a local butcher's shop. This gave me a much greater understanding of the meat we all eat, where it comes from, and how to utilize each part of the animal. I learned a lot while working there, including how to break down a whole animal into its different muscle groups and cuts. Knowing all the different parts of each of the animals gave me so many more ideas for recipes. I understood meat a lot more after working there. I can take that knowledge and understanding forwards in my life and use it to my advantage. I made some great friends while working there as well, and it never hurts to know people who sell really good quality meat.

I have experimented a lot with different meat dishes and different types of meat. I always like to try different things and push my abilities to learn new techniques. The first dish listed below in the meat section is a prime example of this. I had never come across this dish before, and I took what I knew about pan frying different things and what flavour combinations work well together.

I have found that lots of people eat the same things week in week out, and my wife and I have also fallen into this easy way of eating. I like to try and mix it up and eat a variety.

Near the end of the book, I have put in a chart to show the temperature that various foods need to reach to be safe to eat. I always used to use Google to find out what temperature something needed to get to. I found this very annoying when following a recipe, either on my phone, and needing to go backwards and forwards between different pages, or when following a recipe in a book, needing to go to my phone to find out what temperature was needed. I have found having it to hand is very beneficial.

Meat Temperature Chart

INTERNAL TEMPERATURE:

MEAT	RARE	MEDIUM	WELL DONE
CHICKEN	N/A	N/A	74°C 165°F
PORK	N/A	69°C 155°F	71°C 160°F
LAMB	52°C 125°F	60°C 140°F	71°C 160°F
BEEF	52°C 125°F	63°C 145°F	71°C 160°F
DUCK	57°C 135°F	63°C 145°F	74°C 165°F

Different Cuts of Meat

Fillet

The fillet muscle is located alongside the spine of the animal. Being protected on two sides by bone, it is the least used muscle in the body of the animal; this is what makes it so tender. The more the muscle is used throughout the life of the animal, the tougher it is going to be.

The fillet steak is the most tender cut that you can get from any animal and, therefore, the most expensive. The fillet muscle also has the least fat of any of the normal steak cuts. The only fillet that is worth eating as a steak that is readily available is a beef fillet. It is cooked as steaks but is also used to make Beef Wellington. As it is the most tender, it is also the best cut to make steak tartar with.

The tail of the fillet cannot be used very well as a steak or as a roast, as it tapers off so quickly. The best use for it, I find, is to cut it into thin strips and use it in a stir fry. I find it the most tender part of the fillet, and it works very well in stir-fries. It is very hard to find the tail in shops and is much more readily found in butchers' shops. As they can't sell it as easily, you might be able to get it a bit cheaper than the main cut of fillet.

The pork tenderloin is the same cut of meat, just on a smaller scale. This can either be cut into small steaks and fried. More commonly, it is butterflied out with a mixture laid on top and then rolled back up and then roasted in the oven. I have recipes for both different methods in the meat chapter. In my opinion, this is a very underutilise cut of meat and can be picked up very cheap from most large shops.

Sirloin

Just on the other side of the spine is the sirloin muscle. It is larger than the fillet and flatter in shape. It normally has a fat cap running along the top of it, but still little to no fat through the muscle itself.

Sirloin is a much cheaper cut than the fillet, and it is probably the most common cut of steak that you will find in restaurants or shops; for this reason, it is probably the one that most people would go for. The sirloin is still very tender and usually much larger than the fillet due to the size of the muscle. As the sirloin and fillet are connected by the spine, they can be cooked at the same time on the same cut; this is called a T-bone steak. On the right-hand side of the bone is the sirloin, and to the left is the fillet.

 Sirloin can also be boned and rolled into a roasting joint. Using this cut can elevate the Sunday roast to a whole new level. When I used to be a butcher, there were always a lot of orders for rolled sirloin for people's Christmas orders. As it is a more tender cut than the normal topside, which is normally used for a roast, it is best to leave the middle a bit pink, just as you would cook it as a steak.

Away from beef, the sirloin/ribeye muscle is used in a rack of lamb. As this is a much smaller animal, the whole muscle is normally sold as one in the whole rack, with ribeye on one end and the sirloin on the other. The picture is of the ribeye and the sirloin, the sirloin on the left and the ribeye on the right. It is rare that you see a rack of lamb that hasn't been French-trimmed, as this is what people are used  to, and it looks a lot smarter. This cut can be cooked all the way through to well done, but it is more tender when it is cooked to medium.

When it comes to pork, the sirloin is normally simply called a pork loin steak or pork medallion, or when the bone is left in, they are referred to as pork chops. Pork chops can also be the ribeye end of the muscle as well. The loin of pork can also be roasted bone-in or boned and rolled. The skin can be left on to create crackling. You should be able to pick one of these up from most butchers. Depending on the size of the one you want, you may have to pre-order it.

Ribeye

The ribeye and sirloin are one long muscle, with sirloin on one side and ribeye on the other

end. The ribeye section is the front part of the muscle and is fattier than the sirloin, with a section of fat that separates the two different muscles that make up the cut. As there is more fat in it, it is worth cooking it for longer than you would a fillet or a sirloin. If you like your fillet or sirloin rare, then it would be worth cooking a ribeye to a medium, as this will mean that more of the fat will render out, and in my opinion, taste better. If you prefer a fattier cut of steak, then this is the one to go for, in my opinion. It is normally a bit more expensive than the sirloin, but not as expensive as the fillet.

Further up the muscle, the ribeye turns into the rib roast, which is normally cooked on the bone. It is also often French-trimmed to make it look more impressive. The one in the picture is one that I prepared when I was working as a butcher. This cut contains the ribeye muscle with the rib cap on top of it. I think that this is the king of all roasting joints and, if cooked right, will be one of the best pieces of meat you will eat.

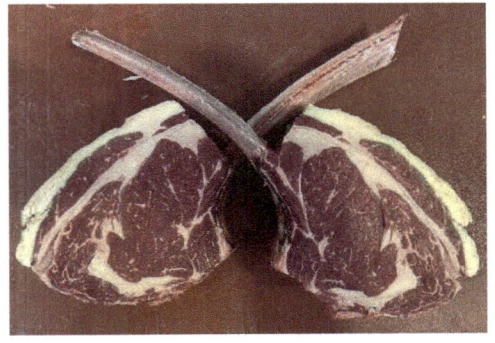

Pork ribeyes are very similar to beef in that they can be fried as a steak or they can be tied and roasted. Unlike beef, you need to make sure that you cook pork all the way through to make sure that it is safe to eat. Pork shoulder steak can also work very well in the slow cooker to make pulled pork. If you use steaks to make pulled pork, then the pieces of meat will be shorter. If you are after the longer pieces of meat when making pulled pork, then it is better to use large pieces of pork shoulder.

Rump

The rump steak is located just behind the sirloin towards to back of the animal. The two best uses for this cut are to fry it as a steak or to tie it up and roast it. The rump steak is a very underrated cut of meat, in my opinion. It is the cheapest of the common steaks that you can buy. It is slightly tougher than the sirloin but can still make for a very nice steak. It has a very similar amount of fat

to the sirloin with a fat cap on top of the muscle, with most of the muscle being very lean. As a roast, it is not one that everyone knows about.

This is the same for lambs and pigs as well, but it is not common in a supermarket, and you will most likely need to go to a butcher's shop and place a special order.

Topside / Silverside

This cut is located at the very back of the animal. Its primary use is to be used in roasts and is the most likely cut you will be getting if you go to a supermarket and get a 'roasting joint.' The more the muscle is used by the animal, the tougher it will be and the cheaper it will be.

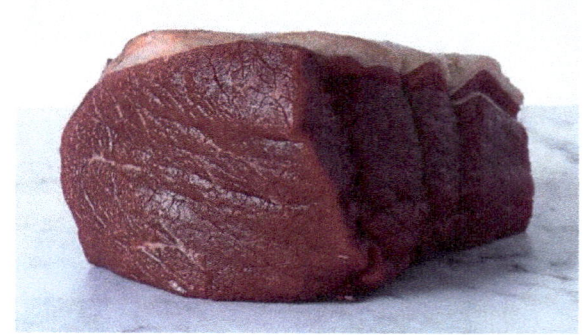

Shin

Most people are not aware of just how delicious this cut can be. It is one of the most used muscles in the animal, so it is very tough and has of connective tissue. The best way to cook this

is with either a slow cooker or in a slow-cooked stew. If it is cooked low and slow, the connective tissue has a chance to break down, and the meat releases all that flavour into the stew. If you can get it with the bone in, then the marrow will also go into the stew, and that has incredible flavour.

Brisket

This muscle is located at the bottom of the front of the animal. Like the shin, it tastes best when it is cooked low and slow. One of the most popular ways to cook it is to smoke it. This process takes a very long time, but when done right is incredibly tasty.

Pork Tenderloin Medallions

FEEDS 2

This is the most tender cut of pork and, in my opinion, very much worth the time that this dish takes to make. These are classic flavours that never go a miss and were a bit hit the first time that I cooked the dish. This dish works very well with mashed potatoes on page 141 and steamed tender stem broccoli.

Ingredients:

- 1 whole pork tenderloin
- 100g cornflour
- 1tsp rosemary
- 1tsp thyme
- 250ml apple juice

Method:

- In a frying pan, put enough oil in to cover the bottom with about ½ a cm of oil and put on a medium heat.
- In a small saucepan, add the apple and put it on a low heat. Reduce this until you get a maple syrup texture. This should take 20 minutes or so.
- In the meantime, mix the cornflour, rosemary, and thyme on a plate or in a bowl.
- Cut the pork tenderloin into 1cm-thick steaks.
- Place the pork steaks in the cornflour and make sure that the whole steak is covered in the cornflour.
- Put 1tsp of the cornflour into the apple juice; this will help the sauce thicken.
- Put the pork into the oil, and as it cooks, there should be small bubbles around the outside. If there are large bubbles, turn the heat down.
- Cook the pork for 5 minutes and then flip it over and cook for 5 minutes on the other side.
- Once cooked, take the steaks out and put them on a wire rack or paper towel to let any excess oil drip off.
- Plate up and drizzle the thickened apple sauce over the top.

Stuffed Pork Tenderloin
FEEDS 4 WITH SIDES

Pork tenderloin is a very underrated cut of meat, which you can get very cheaply from the supermarket. It does require some prep work, but it is worth it.

Ingredients:

- 1 whole pork tenderloin
- 100g baby spinach
- 300g minced chestnut mushrooms
- 100ml apple juice
- Salt and pepper
- 1tbsp butter

Method:

- Preheat the oven to 180 °C.
- Add the mushrooms into a large frying pan with the butter on a low heat for 5-10 minutes or until they have softened. Add in the spinach and wilt it down.
- Stir in the apple juice and spread the mixture out so that it evenly covers the bottom of the frying pan. Let it cook on a low heat until the apple juice has been completely absorbed and the mixture has started drying out.
- While this is reducing, trim both ends off the tenderloin so that you are left with just the thick and even centre section.
- Butterfly it by cutting just along one side of it, around ½ a cm thick. Make the cut along the whole length of the tenderloin. As you make these cuts, roll the meat so that it stays the same thickness. Continue the cutting and rolling until you have one flat piece of meat.
- Sprinkle salt and pepper on one side of the pork, and then once the mushrooms and spinach mixture has no moisture left, spread it out evenly on the pork, leaving ½ a cm of space around all edges of the meat.
- Tightly roll the meat and place it on a sheet of tinfoil. Roll up tightly and place in the oven.
- Cook for 15 minutes or until the pork has reached an internal temperature of 64 °C–67 °C
- Take out of the oven and let it rest for 10 minutes, still wrapped in the tinfoil.

I have served mine with couscous, cauliflower, and broccoli.

Homemade Honey Mustard Ham

While growing up, I was a very fussy eater and pretty much had a ham sandwich every day for lunch at school for around 6 years. I wanted to try and recreate the ham that I used to eat, but improved.

Ingredients:

- 1kg gammon joint
- 2tbsp runny honey
- 2tbsp mustard (I like to use slightly spicy mustard)
- Splash of water

Method:

- Preheat the oven to 180 °C.
- Mix the honey and mustard together in a separate bowl and add the water until it is a thin sauce.
- If you have a meat injector, inject 3 syringes full of the honey mustard sauce into the joint and then, using a basting brush, put a thin layer on top of the joint and place in the roasting tin, cover with tin foil, and place in the oven. If you do not have a syringe to inject, just baste the outside before putting in the oven.
- Cook at 180 °C for 1 hour.
- After 45 minutes, remove the tin foil and baste the joint with the leftover sauce and place it back in the oven, uncovered.
- Re-baste the joint every 10-15 minutes until it has finished cooking.
- The internal temperature should be 68 °C (155 °F). This should take 45 minutes once the foil has been removed, so a total cooking time of around 1 hour and 30 minutes.
- If you are happy that the middle of the joint has reached 68 °C before this time, then take it out, as you do not want it to dry out.
- If you are using it for sandwiches, wait for the joint to completely cool down, and then slice as thin as possible.
- If you are eating it hot, make nice thick slices and enjoy.

Baby Back Ribs

1 FULL RACK PER PERSON

This is a recipe that needs a bit of forethought, as it will take a long time to cook properly in the sous vide. If you do not have a sous vide, then it can be done in an oven.

Ingredients

- Rack of baby back ribs
- 2tbsp dark brown sugar
- 2tsp paprika
- 3tbsp apple juice
- 1tbsp honey
- 2tbsp barbeque sauce

Method

- To prep the ribs, remove the membrane from the underside of the ribs by getting the tip of a knife under the membrane on one end. Pull the membrane off from one side to the other. It will look a bit like a layer of skin.
- Mix the dark brown sugar, paprika, apple juice, honey, and barbeque sauce in a bowl and rub all over the ribs.
- If you are using a sous vide, seal in a vacuum pack and place in the water bath set at 65 °C and cook for up to 24 hours. If you do not have that much time, then anything over 12 will work as well. The longer you have, the more tender they will be. To get a good seal, you may need to cover the ends of the bones with tin foil, as they may poke a hole in the bag. You may also need to cut the rack of ribs in half to fit it in the bag.
- If you are not using a sous vide, you can wrap the ribs in 2-3 layers of tin foil and place them in an oven at 140 °C for 4-6 hours.
- The ribs can just simply be put on the barbecue, but they will not be as juicy and tender.
- Once out of the sous vide or oven, finish them on the barbecue to get a nice sear.

Tomahawk Steak
FEEDS 2 WITH SIDES

This is one of the most impressive things you can cook, in my opinion, both in looks and taste. There are a few different ways you can cook it. I will cover a couple of them. The ingredients list is very short, as I think the taste of the steak itself does the talking, but there is not a lot that isn't improved with garlic butter.

Ingredients

- 1 tomahawk steak
- 2tbsp garlic butter

Method 1 – Barbecue/Frying Pan

- Straight on the barbecue or frying pan on medium heat, cook until it has reached your desired internal temperature; the chart for this can be found on page 53.
- Allow it to cook for at least 5 minutes on one side without flipping it to ensure you develop a good crust.
- If you are cooking it in a frying pan, put the garlic butter in with the steak and baste it to help the flavour penetrate the steak.
- Take it off and let it rest for at least 10 minutes before slicing.

Method 2 – Reverse Sear

- Preheat the oven to 180 °C.
- In a high-heat pan, sear the steak on all sides to seal in the flavour.
- Put in the oven on a wire rack for 35-60 minutes, depending on the thickness of the steak and how well done you want it. The best way to ensure you achieve your desired cook is to use a meat thermometer.
- If the steak is a normal size, around 1 ½-2 cm and around 1kg. 35 minutes for very rare and 60 minutes for well done.
- Take it out and let it rest for at least 10 minutes before slicing.

Pulled Pork Parcels
2 PARCELS PER PERSON

This is great for meal prep, but works incredibly well as part of a bigger meal. It's also a great way to use up some leftover pulled pork.

Ingredients:

- 200g self-raising flour
- 150g Greek yogurt
- 150g pulled pork (a recipe for this can be found on page 153)
- 1 diced jalapeno
- Grated cheddar or mozzarella

Method:

- Mix the flour and Greek yogurt together until dough clumps form. Dust the counter with flour and start kneading the dough until it becomes smooth.
- Separate the dough into 4 pieces and form them into ball shapes.
- Using a rolling pin, roll them flat until they are thin and you can start to see the light through them.
- In the centre of each dough base, place a tbsp of pulled pork (make sure that the pulled pork does not have too much excess juice) and top with grated cheese and jalapenos, leaving roughly 1.5cm of dough around the outside.
- Taking the opposite side, meet them in the middle, and continue this process all the way around until there is no longer any of the pulled pork.
- Gently press down on the top of the ball until it is flat and around 1 cm thick.
- Place in a dry frying pan on a very low heat and cook for 5 minutes on each side, flipping every 2.5 minutes. It is cooked when each side is golden brown.
- Place on a plate and cut 4 pieces into each parcel, and dip into the gravy made from the juices of the pulled pork.

Steak Sandwich

FEEDS 2

When I first made this for my wife, I was told that it was one of the nicest things she had ever eaten and asked if we could do it every week. It can take some patience with the caramelised onions, but it is worth it.

Ingredients:

2 steaks
- ½ a small baguette per person
- Balsamic glaze
- Chilli oil (optional)
- A handful of fresh rocket
- 1 onion per person
- Red wine vinegar
- Salt and pepper
- Whole bulb of garlic
- 200g butter

Method:

- Preheat the oven to 170 degrees, cut the top off the garlic and drizzle with oil, and wrap in tin foil. Place the garlic in the oven and cook for 30 minutes.
- Slice the onion into thin slices and put it into a large frying pan on a high heat with a dash of oil. Stir so that they cook evenly.
- When they start to get some colour, turn the heat all the way down, and if the onions start to stick, deglaze with a small splash of the red wine vinegar. Cook until they have caramelised; this could take up to 30 minutes. Try and remain patient, as turning up the heat will just make them crispy and not achieve the classic caramelised onion flavour.
- Once you are happy with the onions, take them out and set them to one side.
- Take the garlic out of the oven and unwrap it from the tin foil. You should be able to squeeze the garlic into a bowl. Add the softened butter and mix well. If the garlic taste is too strong, add some more butter until the desired taste is reached.
- Sprinkle salt and pepper on each side of the steak and put in the same frying pan with a big tsp of butter. Cook the steaks until they have reached the required level (for me, this is a ribeye steak at medium).
- Butter each side of the bread with the garlic butter layer on top, the rocket drizzle of balsamic glaze, and chilli oil. Slice the steak on the angle, put it on top, and place the top half of the bread to complete the sandwich.

Bolognese Risotto
FEEDS 4

If you like the taste of bolognese but want a different way of serving it, then this is a great alternative. There are two different ways of doing this recipe: you can do it with the normal bolognese recipe, or you can upgrade it using the Beef Ragu recipe.

This is option one: Normal Bolognese.

Ingredients:

- 2 large carrots/3 medium carrots
- 3 sticks of celery
- 1 white onion
- 3 tbsp butter
- 4 cloves of garlic, minced
- 500g beef mince
- 1 beef stock cube (I like to use a stock pot)
- 200ml red wine
- 500g bolognese sauce
- 350g risotto rice
- Cheese of choice (My wife likes cheddar, but Parmesan can also work)

Method:

- Peel and finely dice the carrots, celery, and onion, along with butter, and put in a large frying pan on a low heat. Place a lid on the frying pan, stirring every couple of minutes to make sure everything is cooking evenly.
- Cook for 5 minutes, and then add in the minced garlic and cook for an additional 15 minutes.
- Add in the mince and break it up so that it's in small pieces.
- Add the salt and pepper and red wine. Leave the lid off and cook until the liquid has been absorbed.
- Add the bolognese sauce and use 300ml of water to get the last of the sauce out of the jar.
- Add the stock cube, mix everything together well, and start cooking the pasta.
- Put the lid on the frying pan until the stock cube has fully dissolved, and then take the lid off and reduce the liquid until the sauce has thickened.
- Add the risotto rice and mix in well so that it is evenly distributed in the sauce.
- Add in 300ml of beef stock and stir into the sauce until it has all been absorbed by the rice and sauce. Repeat this process until the rice has finished cooking. This should be 600ml-900ml of beef stock.

Beef Ragu Risotto

FEEDS 4

This dish is very similar to the Beef Ragu with Tagliatelle on page 35, but substituting the pasta for risotto, and you have a very easy way to potentially utilize leftovers. You will need a slow cooker for this recipe.

Ingredients:

- 500g beef (I prefer a fattier cut like chuck, but lean also works well)
- 3tbsp tomato puree
- 2 beef stock cubes
- 700ml water
- 2 large carrots
- 3 sticks of celery
- 400g tin of chopped tomatoes
- Salt and black pepper
- 200ml red wine
- 600ml-900ml beef stock

Method

- In a slow cooker, put the diced beef, roughly chopped carrots, roughly chopped celery, tomato puree, water, red wine, and beef stock cubes and season with salt and pepper and stir well. Put the slow cooker on high for 5 hours or on low for 8 hours, depending on how much time you have. Stir every hour or so to make sure that everything is mixed well.
- Once the beef easily falls apart, pick out all the pieces and, on a separate plate, shred them.
- Put the rest of the contents of the slow cooker in a blender and blend on the slowest speed for 30 seconds–1 minute. It is done when the pieces of celery and carrot are the size of chocolate chips.
- Place this mixture into a large high-sided frying pan or saucepan and place on medium heat so that it is gently bubbling, and the sauce starts to reduce. Add the shredded beef back into the sauce and stir well so that it is evenly distributed.
- As the sauce is reducing, start cooking your pasta and season the sauce to taste with salt and pepper.
- Once it has reached the desired consistency, add the risotto rice and mix well so that it is evenly distributed in the sauce.
- Add in 300ml of beef stock and stir into the sauce until it has all been absorbed by the rice and sauce. Repeat this process until the rice has finished cooking. This should be 600ml-900ml of beef stock.

Rack of lamb

FEEDS 2 WITH SIDES

I find this is a great meal for a special occasion. I am preparing this meal for Valentine's Day, which is coming up in a few days as I am writing this. I will be serving this with the Pomme Anna on page 135 and steamed greens.

Ingredients:

- 1 full rack of lamb—usually 7 or 8 bones
- 1 finely minced bulb of garlic
- 5tbsp of oil
- 1tbsp dried or fresh rosemary
- Salt and black pepper
- 1tbsp dried mint
- 2tsp melted butter

Method:

- Put all the ingredients except the lamb in a large ziplock bag and mix well.
- Score the fat cap on the outside of the rack so that the flavour can penetrate the meat.
- Remove the thin membrane from the underside of the bones.
- Put the rack of lamb in the bag with the mixed-up ingredients and get as much air out of the bag as possible before sealing. Place it in the fridge and marinate for 24-48 hours before cooking.
- Preheat the oven to 200 °C.
- Sear the lamb in a high heat frying pan on all sides and then transfer it into the oven and cook depending on how you like it cooked.
- Take it out of the oven, cover it in foil, and let it rest for 10 minutes before carving.
- 20 minutes for rare—internal temperature of 125 Fahrenheit–52 °Celsius
- 25 minutes for medium rare—internal temperature of 135 Fahrenheit–57.2 °Celsius
- 30 minutes for medium—internal temperature of 140 Fahrenheit–60 °Celsius
- Bear in mind that the temperature of the meat will rise when resting.
- I use a meat thermometer to keep track of the meat while it is cooking to make sure that I don't overcook it.

Stock

Making your own stock is a great but simple way to enhance the flavours of your dishes.

Ingredients:

- One of the following:
    1. Giblets from a duck, goose, chicken, or turkey
    2. Carcass of duck, goose, chicken, or turkey
    3. Beef, pork, or lamb bones, preferably with some meat still on them
- 2 large carrots, roughly chopped
- 3 sticks of celery, roughly chopped
- Salt
- Pepper
- Star anise (optional)

Method:

- If the meat element of the stock is raw, then heat up a large saucepan over the stove and place the meat in it with a dash of oil. Cook, turning every now and again, until all sides of it are browned and a fond is left on the bottom of the pan.
- Add 1.5-2 litres of water into the pan along with the carrots and celery, both roughly chopped.
- Add a heavy pinch of salt and pepper into the pot and bring to a boil.
- Turn the heat down so that the mixture is simmering with the lid on and leave it for 1 hour and 30 minutes–2 hours, stirring occasionally to prevent anything from sticking to the bottom.
- Once the time has elapsed, use a fine sieve to strain the liquid into another pot. Complete this process 3-4 times to make sure that everything has been strained out.
- Cool this liquid down, and if it is not going to be used soon, then it can be frozen for use in the future.

Italian Sushi

I saw this recipe go viral online and had to try it for myself. It is quite fiddly, but I think worth the effort. Most of the ingredients in this recipe can be adjusted depending on how much you like each one.

Ingredients:

- 10 slices prosciutto ham
- I handful of rockets
- 50g sundried tomato
- 1 sliced tomato
- ½ a ball of mozzarella, sliced
- 5 thin slices of chorizo
- 5 thin slices of salami
- Balsamic glaze

Method:

- Separate the slices of prosciutto and place them with just one edge overlapping on a piece of cling film.
- Spread the rest of the ingredients about 1/3 of the way down the ham.
- As tightly as you can, roll up from the top into a tight 'sushi roll.'
- To help the roll keep its form, roll tightly in the cling film and place in the fridge for as long as you can before cutting. (Preferably overnight, but 1 hour should be alright.)
- Cut into 1 cm rolls and place on a plate.
- Drizzle the balsamic glaze over the top.

Tangy Salmon

FEEDS 2

This dish is a very fresh and tasty way to serve salmon, which might be a bit different from what you are used to doing. It is very easy to do and is a brilliant mid-week meal

Ingredients:

- 2cm ginger/2tsp minced ginger
- 2tbsp soy sauce
- 1tbsp runny honey
- 4 cloves minced garlic/1tsp garlic powder
- 1 salmon fillet per person

Method:

- Skin and dice the ginger as finely as you can and place in a bowl. Add in the honey, minced garlic, and soy sauce.
- Mix well and put the salmon in the mixture, and marinate for 30 minutes before cooking. Place the salmon skin side down in the oven or air fryer at fryer at 180 °C for 12-15 minutes. Drizzle the remainder of the sauce over the salmon before cooking.
- Once the salmon is cooked, scrape off any excess ginger from the top.

Lemon and Garlic Prawns

This is a great little side that can be cooked well on the barbecue or in the kitchen.

Ingredients:

6 large prawns

- The juice of half a lemon
- 4 minced cloves of garlic
- 4tbsp oil
- 1tbsp grated hard cheese such as Parmesan or Pecorino Romano

Method:

- Mix the lemon juice, garlic, oil, and Parmesan in a bowl.
- Put 4-5 prawns on a skewer and brush both sides of the prawns with the mix.
- Place on the barbecue, frying pan, or air fryer on high heat and cook for 3-5 minutes. Then flip over and re-baste, and cook for another 3-5 minutes.
- If the prawns are raw, they will be grey and will turn pink when they are cooked.
- Once they are cooked, re-baste the prawns again.

Grilled Octopus

This dish may seem a bit intimidating, but it is one of the easiest dishes in this book. The hardest bit of it is the very beginning, which is cutting it up properly.

Ingredients:

- One whole octopus
- Zest and juice of 1 lemon
- Salt and pepper
- Butter
- Sides (I prefer to do it with steamed broccoli and homemade chips with tzatziki to dip the octopus in)

Method:

- Clean the octopus. And if the fishmonger has not already done so, remove the entrails and eyes.
- The easiest way I found to do this was to turn the head inside out, and you will be able to see the entrails, which are in a sack attached to the underside of the head. Using a sharp knife, cut the bits of connecting tissue to separate the entrails from the head. Once the entrails are off, the head should look like a deflated balloon with the bottom cut off. Turn the head back the right way so it's not inside out anymore. To remove the eyes, cut around them and down around 1 cm or so to make sure that you get the whole thing.
- Wash the tentacles, making sure to get in each of the suckers. Turn the tentacles over, and where they all meet, you will see a small spot of black; this is the beak. You can remove this by simply pushing it out from the other side. If it is being stubborn, then it is easy enough to cut around and pop out.
- The octopus can be eaten with the skin on; however, if you choose to remove it, run a sharp knife down each tentacle to expose the flesh underneath. Get your thumb underneath the skin, and you should be able to peel it off. This technique should work for the rest of the body as well.
- Bring a pot of water to a boil and then reduce the heat to a simmer. Season it with the lemon zest and the salt and pepper. Place the octopus in the simmering water, place a lid on the pot, and leave it for 45-60 minutes until you can pierce the thickest part of the body with a knife without too much resistance. Once you are happy that it is done, take it out, cut the head off, and cut in between the tentacles so that you are left with just 8 pieces and the head. The head can then be sliced width-wise to create rings.
- Place the pieces in a frying pan with a splash of oil on high heat for 5 – 10 minutes until golden.

Octopus and Potato Salad

All the steps for prepping and cooking the octopus are in the previous recipe for grilled octopus. So, in this one, I am focusing on the other aspects to make it into the salad.

Ingredients:

Tentacles of one whole octopus
- 350g peeled and diced new potatoes
- 1 lemon
- 2 finely sliced spring onions
- 4tbsp mayo
- 1tsp mustard

Method:

Cook the octopus using the lime as described in the previous recipe. While it is cooking, start with the potatoes.
- Put a pot of water on the boil.
- Peel the potatoes and cut into quarters, and boil for 15 minutes until you can cut them easily with a sharp knife.
- Strain the potatoes and set to one side.
- Once the octopus is cooked, cut the tentacles in half and put them in a frying pan with a splash of oil.
- In a separate bowl, mix the mayonnaise, lemon juice, and mustard.
- Once the octopus is grilled, add the potatoes to the frying pan and cook for 5 minutes until the octopus gets a bit of colour.
- Put the potatoes and octopus in a bowl and add 2-4 tbsp of the sauce into the bowl, along with the spring onion.
- Mix everything together so that there is an even coating of sauce on everything.

Poultry

Staples

This section has a huge range of different dishes, from quick and easy fried chicken to crispy shredded duck, which takes hours and lots of hard work. Both can be cooked wrong and taste bad or tough, but when cooked right, they will be amazingly tasty. Some of these recipes may already be part of your repertoire, and there may be some that can be added to it.

Crispy Shredded Duck and Pancakes

FEEDS 4

My wife always gets this when we get a takeaway so I tried to replicate it as best I can. It's a labour of love and takes a bit of time and attention, but according to my wife, it is definitely worth it.

Ingredients:

- A whole duck
- Salt
- Pepper
- Chinese 5-spice

For Pancakes:

- 150g plain flour
- 125ml boiling water
- 1/3 of a cucumber
- 2 spring onions
- Hoisin sauce

Method:

- Preheat the oven to 160 °C and pat the duck dry with kitchen roll. Sprinkle salt, pepper, and Chinese 5-spice all over the duck top and bottom. Put the duck in the oven and cook for 3 hours and 30 minutes. Turn the duck every hour so that it cooks evenly.
- While the duck is cooking, prepare the pancakes by weighing 150g of plain flour and adding 125ml of boiling water with a heavy pinch of salt. Stir the mixture with a wooden spoon until it is cool enough to knead by hand. Dust the work surface with flour so that it doesn't stick. Turn the dough out onto the work surface and knead it into a small ball; this takes around 10 minutes.
- Divide the dough into 12 even-sized balls. Keep the work surface dusted with flour so that it doesn't stick. Using a floured rolling pin, roll out the balls as evenly as possible and as thin as you can.
- To cook the pancakes, heat up a non-stick frying pan on medium heat and put each pancake in individually and cook on the flat side for around 20-30 seconds.
- Cut the cucumber into thin batons and set to one side.
- Thinly slice the spring onions on a bias
- Once the duck has been cooked, take it out of the oven and shred the whole thing with 2 forks.
- Place a bit of everything on a pancake, wrap it up, and enjoy.

Teriyaki Chicken and Rice

FOR 4 PEOPLE

This is a very easy way to change up the weekly meal and a great way to get close to replicating a takeaway.

Ingredients:

- 300g white rice
- 2 chicken breasts
- 2 romano peppers
- 50ml soy sauce
- 30ml sesame oil (sunflower or vegetable oil also works)
- 5tbsp brown sugar
- 3cm finely diced fresh ginger/3 tsp ginger paste
- 2tsp chilli flakes
- 50ml rice vinegar
- 4 spring onions
- Sesame seeds (optional)

Method:

- To prepare the rice, start by washing the rice, straining it off, and putting enough water in so there is 1 cm of water above the rice. Bring it to the boil and cook for 7 minutes with the lid on. Then turn the heat off and let it steam cook—do not remove the lid for at least 10-15 minutes.

- While the rice is cooking, slice the peppers and add them to a frying pan and cook on a medium heat for 7 minutes until they start to soften. Slice the chicken into thin pieces and add them to the frying pan with the peppers and cook until they start to brown.

- In a separate bowl, add in the soy sauce, sesame oil, brown sugar, finely diced fresh ginger/3tsp ginger paste, chilli flakes, and rice vinegar. Mix all together well and add to the frying pan. Reduce the heat and stir well until the sauce thickens and becomes sticky.

- Portion the rice and add the teriyaki chicken and top with the slices of spring onions and optional sesame seeds.

Marinated Chicken Breasts

This recipe can be used for any cut of chicken, but I find that the thickness of the chicken breast allows time for the chicken to develop a lovely sticky caramelised crust. This can be had as a main with some veg and carbohydrate, such as chips or rice. It can also work well sliced up on some pasta.

Ingredients

- 2 chicken breasts
- 4tbsp dark soy sauce
- 4tbsp honey
- 5 cloves minced garlic
- 2tsp minced ginger/2cm finely grated ginger
- 1tsp harissa paste
- Black pepper

Method:

- To make the marinade, combine the soy sauce, honey, minced garlic, minced ginger, harissa paste, and black pepper in a bowl and mix well until completely mixed.
- Transfer the marinade into a sealable bag, such as a zip lock or tieable sandwich bag, and add in the chicken breasts.
- Set this aside in the fridge for as long as you can wait. 24 hours is ideal, but if you only have 30 minutes–1 hour, that works well, too.
- Place the chicken into a frying pan on medium heat with a splash of oil and put a lid on the frying pan. Every few minutes, move the chicken to mop up the sauce as it starts to thicken. Turn the chicken every time so that the sauce is spread over the chicken evenly.
- Once all the sauce has been mopped up, this should take around 10–15 minutes. Place in the air fryer or oven at 180 °C to finish cooking. This will vary depending on how thick the chicken breast is. The chicken is cooked when you have reached an internal temperature of between 70 and 75 degrees.

Soy, Honey, and Orange Roast Duck

Roast duck is a great alternative to a Sunday roast or for a special occasion.

Ingredients:

- Whole duck 1.8-2kg
- 3tbsp soy sauce
- 3tbsp orange juice
- 2tbsp honey
- 1 whole orange

Method:

- Preheat the oven to 200 °C.
- In a bowl, mix together the soy sauce, orange juice, and honey.
- Using a basting brush, coat the exterior of the duck in the sauce.
- Place the duck on a wire rack in the oven and cook for 30 minutes.
- After 30 minutes, take the duck out of the oven and re-baste and turn the oven down to 150 °C and place the duck back in the oven.
- Cook for another 2-2.5 hours, re-basting every 30 minutes.
- Each time you baste with the sauce mixture, pour over any fat that has collected in the bottom of the roasting tin.
- Once it has cooked, take it out of the oven and let it rest for 10 minutes before carving.

Chicken Bites

This is a great little addition to a lot of meals, can be used as a side or can be used as a substitute in the chicken wraps recipe on page 113.

Ingredients:

Chicken:

- Chicken breasts or thighs
- 500g flour
- 300g cornflour
- 2tbsp paprika
- Salt and pepper
- 2tsp chilli flakes (optional)
- Fizzy drink (I use either beer or cider, but sparkling water also works well)

- Oil

Optional sauce:

- 2 cloves of minced garlic
- 3tbsp soy sauce
- 3tbsp honey
- 200ml water
- 1tsp cornflour

Method:

- Cut the chicken into small strips. If you are using chicken breasts, then it is best to butterfly them first and then cut them into strips. But if you are using thighs, then just cutting into strips width-ways works well.
- To make the wet batter, add half the flour, cornflour, paprika, and chilli flakes to a large bowl, and add the fizzy drink until it is the same consistency as a very thin pancake batter.
- To make the dry mix, add the other half of the ingredients to another bowl, minus the fizzy drink, along with a generous seasoning with salt and pepper, and mix well.
- Dip each piece of chicken in the wet batter and then into the dry, and then repeat. So, each piece of chicken will go into each bowl twice.
- Heat an inch of oil in a medium heat frying pan for 5 minutes, and then in batches, place the battered chicken into the oil. Cook for 7 minutes on each side or until it is golden brown.
- Remove from the oil and let it to dry on a wire rack.

Optional sauce:

- In a separate frying pan, put the minced garlic, soy sauce, and honey, and in a separate bowl, mix the water and cornflour. Add this mixture into the pan and cook on a low heat until the sauce and thickened and reduced.
- Coat the chicken with the sauce and enjoy.

Fried Chicken Burgers

Chicken burgers make a great alternative to getting a takeaway, and in my opinion, taste a lot better. When cooking fakeaway meals at home, you also know what goes into it, and it can be a much healthier option

Ingredients:

- 1 chicken breast per person
- 50g crushed cornflakes
- ½ tsp Chinese five-spice
- 1 tsp garlic powder
- A large pinch of salt and pepper
- 1tsp paprika
- Oil for cooking
- Smooth mustard, such as English
- 1 burger bun per person
- Slice of cheese
- Sauce of choice
- Crisp lettuce

Method:

- Crush the cornflakes so that they are a coarse powder consistency. In a flat bowl, mix in the Chinese five-spice, paprika, salt, and pepper with the crushed cornflakes.
- Butterfly the chicken breast out flat and coat entirely in the mustard, and then place each chicken breast in the cornflake mix and make sure that the whole thing is completely coated and press down so that pieces will not flake off easily.
- Put a frying pan on medium heat with a dash of oil. Place the chicken breast in the frying pan and cook for 5 minutes on each side, keep turning the chicken breasts every 5 minutes until the outside is golden brown and it is cooked all the way through. This should take 3-4 flips for a total cooking time of 15-20 minutes.
- Take the chicken breasts out and place them to one side. Lightly toast the burger bun and then assemble with the lettuce, sauce, cheese, and chicken breast.
- Serve with a side of chips.

Pan-Fried Chicken

This very quick and easy dish is a great way to put a twist on a regular fried chicken breast.

Ingredients:

- 1 chicken breast per person
- 100g plain flour
- 1tsp paprika
- A large pinch of salt and pepper
- 3tbsp butter

Method:

- Put the flour, paprika, salt, and pepper into a flat bowl and mix well.
- Butterfly the chicken breast in half so that both halves are even.
- Coat all sides of the chicken breasts in the seasoned flour.
- Melt the butter in a frying pan and place the coated chicken breasts in the frying pan and cook for 5 minutes on each side. Keep turning the chicken breasts every 5 minutes until the outside is golden brown and it is cooked all the way through. This should take 3-4 flips. For a total cooking time of 15-20 minutes.

Chicken Wraps

FEEDS 6-8

This dish does not take a lot of time to cook or prepare and can be very easily changed to suit all different taste buds.

Ingredients:

- 500g of sliced chicken breasts or thighs
- 3 bell peppers
- 2 onions
- Fresh grated cheese
- Shredded lettuce/preprepared bag of salad – roughly 100g
- 8 wraps
- Paprika
- Salt & pepper
- Sunflower/vegetable oil
- Sauces of choice

Method:

- If you are using chicken breasts, butterfly them out and then cut into thin strips lengthwise from top to bottom. If the strips of chicken are too long, then cut them in half to a more manageable size. For chicken thighs, then cut into similar-sized strips lengthwise. Put the chicken in a large frying pan, with a dash of oil on a medium heat. Cook for 5 minutes, stirring regularly.
- Cut the bell peppers into the same shape length ways into long strips, and then add these into the same frying pan and mix well, cooking for an additional 5 minutes.
- Slice the onion into thin semi-circles and add to the pan. Mix well again to make sure that all the layers of the onion have separated.
- Season with a pinch of salt, a sprinkle of black pepper, and 2 tablespoons of paprika. Mix well and put a lid on the frying pan so that it can cook and steam at the same time. Take the lid off and stir every few minutes to stop it from sticking. It is ready when the ingredients are cooked. While this is cooking, there is time to prepare the other ingredients.
- Shred enough lettuce for the wraps you are using, roughly 100 g.
- Great enough cheese for each wrap, depending on how much people like it.
- Assemble the wraps with all the desired ingredients and sauces.

Lemon & Garlic Roast Chicken

FEEDS 4 WITH SIDES

This is always one of my staples for a Sunday roast. It's great for just me and my wife with some leftovers or for the whole family. It's a nice a simple recipe that can be enjoyed by lots of people.

Ingredients:

- A whole chicken 1.5kg-2kg
- 125 grams of salted butter (half a block)
- 4 cloves of garlic
- Juice of half a lemon and the zest of one lemon
- Salt
- Pepper

Method:

- Preheat the oven to 180 °C.
- Soften the butter by either leaving it out of the fridge or by putting it in the microwave for 30 seconds.
- Mince the garlic and add it to the softened butter.
- Juice half the lemon and add this into the butter, along with the zest of the whole lemon.
- Mix the butter well until all the ingredients are incorporated.
- Separate the skin from the meat all over the chicken, doing your best not to break the skin.
- Spread the butter evenly between the meat and the skin all over the chicken.
- Put the leftover lemon in the cavity of the chicken and sprinkle salt and pepper on the whole chicken.
- Put the chicken in the preheated oven in a roasting dish with a wire rack and cook for 40 minutes per kilo, e.g., 1.5kg =1 hour in the oven, 2kg = 1 hour 20 minutes, + 15 minutes or until the meat has reached 75 °C internally.
- Take the chicken out of the oven and leave it to rest for 10-15 minutes.
- Carve and serve with the sides of your choice. (I personally go traditional with roast potatoes, Yorkshire puddings, and cauliflower cheese.)

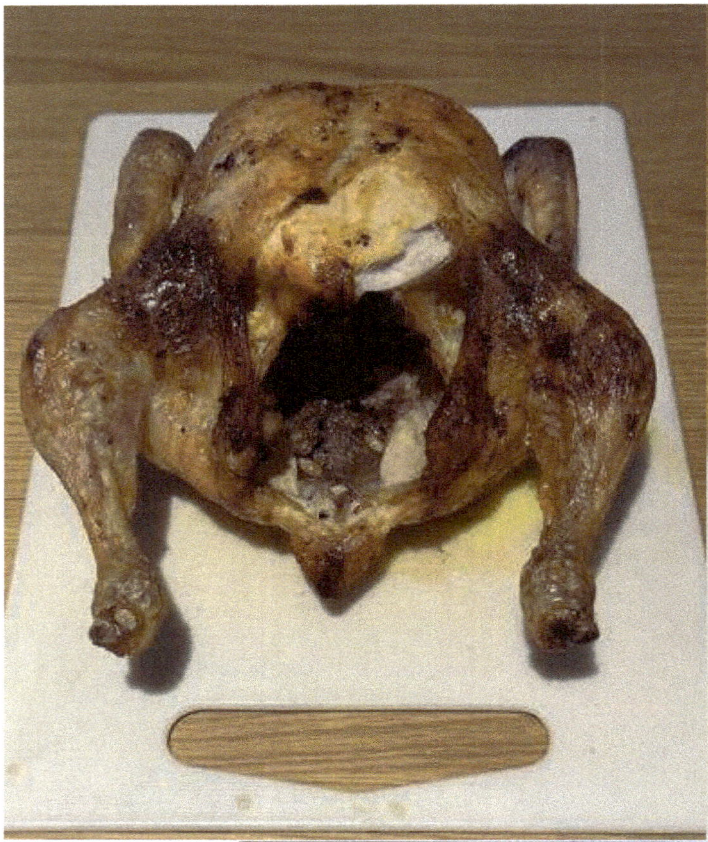

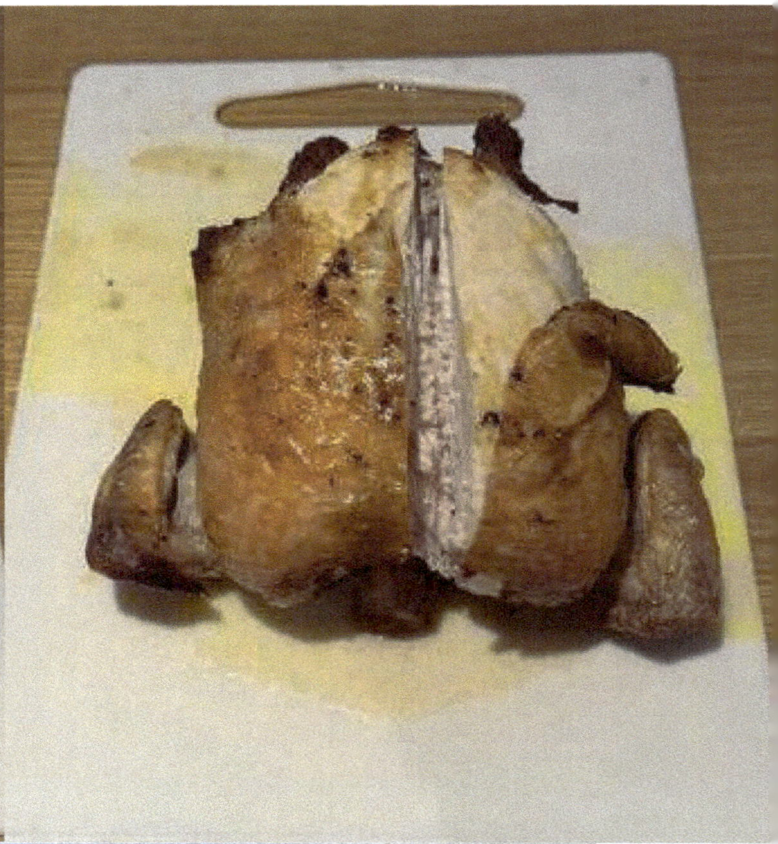

How to Carve a Chicken

Method:

- Make sure that your knife is sharp, as this will make your job a lot easier.

- Face the chicken away from you so that the legs are the end that is closest to you, and cut the skin that separates the drumstick and the main body of the chicken.

- Follow the shape of the chicken down where the thigh meets the body, and you will be able to cut directly through the joint, which will separate the thigh and drumstick.

- Do the same on the other side of the bird.

- Flip the legs so that they are skin side down; there will be a faint line where the drumstick meets the thigh. Cut down this line on an angle, and this will separate the drumstick from the thigh.

- Identify the line between the two breasts and cut down just to one side until you hit the bone, and cut all the way back to the tip of the breast. Follow the shape of the bone down towards the edge of the bird. As you go down and round, you will find the joint for the wing, which will feel the same as the joint between the drumstick and thigh. You can keep this attached to the breast; however, I always choose to separate the two, as this will make carving the breast easier.

- Complete this on the other side of the bird, and you will be left with the carcass, which can be kept to make stock or can be thrown away.

- Turn each chicken breast so that they are side on and then slice on the diagonal.

- The chicken is now a lot easier to serve in order to minimise waste and get as much off the carcass as possible.

Chicken and Halloumi Salad Bowl

When I started losing weight, I did a lot of research into what types of food I should be eating[HS2]. As I really enjoy exciting food that tastes good but is varied, I didn't want to just eat boring salad and chicken.

This is my way of making a salad more exciting and enjoyable to eat. The great thing about these salad bowls is that they can be very easily adapted to suit everyone. To help lower the calories you can reduce the amount of halloumi and replace it with something else.

Ingredients

- Lettuce
- 1 chicken breast/2 chicken thighs per person
- 1 romano pepper
- Half an onion
- 3 slices of halloumi
- Balsamic glaze

Method:

- Start with a base of lettuce, and very thinly slice the onion and pepper, and add them on top.
- Season the chicken with whatever you want. I choose paprika and garlic powder. Put in the air fryer at 180-200 °C and cook for 10 minutes on each side so that it cooks evenly. When you flip the chicken, put the sliced halloumi in the air fryer or frying pan as well, and these should then be done at the same time as the chicken.
- Mix the lettuce, pepper, and onion together and drizzle the balsamic glaze on top.
- Once the chicken is cooked, cut into slices and place on top of the salad with the halloumi.

Potato Fajitas Bowl

This is a great alternative to having a fajita in a wrap in the traditional sense and is another way of hitting it high volume, low calorie, high protein, and high fibre meal. I find this dish works best with a fresh and mild side dish such as steamed broccoli; this helps cut the richness of the dish.

Ingredients:

- 2 medium potatoes per person
- 1 chicken breast per person
- 1 bell/romano pepper per person
- ½ red onion per person
- 100g black beans per person
- Paprika
- Sauce of choice (for me, it's garlic mayo)

Method:

- Dice the potato into 1.5–2 cm cubes, put in the air fryer or oven, spray with oil, and toss with a sprinkle of paprika. Cook for 30 minutes, mixing every 10 minutes to ensure they cook evenly. After 30 minutes, they should be crispy on the outside and fluffy on the inside.

- While the potatoes are cooking, dice up the chicken, red onion, pepper, and paprika and put in a medium heat frying pan and cook for 5 minutes, stirring every 30 seconds or so, until the chicken starts to get a bit of colour.

- Once the chicken has a bit of colour but is not yet cooked all the way through, strain, add in the black beans, and stir to make sure it is evenly distributed. If you can put a lid on the frying pan, cover it, and cook for 10–15 minutes, stirring every couple of minutes to make sure that it doesn't stick to the bottom of the pan.

- Once the chicken is cooked through, the beans are hot, and the peppers and onions have reached the desired texture, mix in the cooked potatoes and plate up, and drizzle with the sauce of your choice.

Lemon Chilli Chicken

It is tart and a bit spicy, but it can be adjusted very easily for spice tolerance by just adding or reducing the amount of chilli flakes. This recipe is for 1 person, and if you want to do it for more people, then just do the same again.

Ingredients:

Juice of one lemon

- 1tsp chilli flakes
- 1tbsp oil
- 1 chicken breast
- 2tbsp butter

Method:

- In a bowl, mix the lemon juice, oil, and chilli flakes.
- Butterfly the chicken breast so that it's nice and flat with a large surface area. Put the chicken in the bowl with the lemon juice mix and let it marinate in the fridge for around an hour or until you lose patience.
- Put the butter in a frying pan on medium–high heat.
- When the butter has melted, add the chicken breast with the excess marinade and cook on one side until you get a nice golden-brown colour, but make sure you flip it before it burns. This should take around 5-10 minutes.
- As the chicken breast cooks on the first side, baste it with the juices in the pan.
- Once the first side is cooked, flip it over and repeat the process.
- Cook for a further 10 minutes.
- The chicken will be cooked when it reaches 74 °C internally.

Chicken Parcels

This is great for meal prep, but works incredibly well as part of a bigger meal.

Ingredients:

- 200g self-raising flour
- 150g Greek yogurt
- 3 boneless, skinless chicken thighs
- 2 romano peppers
- 1 white onion
- 100g frozen peas
- 2tsp Gochujang paste

Method:

- Dice up the chicken thighs, peppers, and onion and add them into a medium heat pan with the gochujang paste and stir well until fully incorporated.
- Cook for 10-15 minutes until the peppers are soft and the chicken is cooked through. Add in the frozen peas and cook for a further 3-5 minutes.
- Mix the flour and Greek yogurt together until dough clumps form. Dust the counter with flour and start kneading the dough until it becomes smooth.
- Separate the dough into 4 pieces and form them into ball shapes.
- Using a rolling pin, roll them flat until they are thin and you can start to see the light through them.
- In the centre of each dough base, place a tablespoon of the chicken mix, leaving roughly 1.5 cm of dough around the outside.
- Taking the opposite side, meet them in the middle, and continue this process all the way around until there is no longer any of the chicken mix.
- Gently press down on the top of the ball until it is flat and around 1cm thick.
- Place in a dry frying pan on a very low heat and cook for 5 minutes on each side. Flipping every 2.5 minutes. It is cooked when each side is golden brown.
- Place on a plate and cut into 4 pieces, and dip into the sauce of your choice.

Stuffed Chicken Breast

This is a very easy way of jazzing up a normal chicken breast and doing something slightly different. All the ingredients in this recipe are for 1 person.

Ingredients:

- 1 chicken breast
- 2 slices of mozzarella
- 3-5 slices of chorizo
- Streaky bacon
- Barbecue sauce

Method:

- Preheat the oven to 180 C.
- Place the chicken breast flat and slice the side of it about ¾ of the way through.
- Fill the gap with the slices of mozzarella, chorizo, and barbecue sauce.
- Wrap bacon around the chicken breast, this will hold it together.
- Bake in the oven for 30 – 40 minutes until done. If you are unsure if it is done, then you can use a temperature probe, and the thickest part should read 74 C.

My Brother

I have learned a lot about food and what we eat from my best friend, Calum. He has a very rare metabolic disorder called Phenylketonuria, or PKU for short. Having this disease means that his body cannot break down protein properly, leading to a very strict day-to-day diet. When we were in primary school, he was limited to around 6 grams of protein a day—which when you stop and really think about it, is such a low amount and is incredibly hard to stick to in a whole day. For example, a plain ham and cheese sandwich from a supermarket has almost 25 grams of protein in it, and a single packet of cheese and onion crisps has 1.6 grams of protein. As he got older, the amount of protein that he had slowly went up, and now, in his late 20s, he can have around 20 grams of protein.

The consequences of going over the amount of protein, especially when he was younger, were severe. If he consistently went over the limit, then he would get bad 'brain fog.' It would severely impact how his brain developed and could potentially stunt his mental growth.

I remember once trying to stick to his diet for a day, and I had to give up by lunchtime as I had already gone over the limit, and he must think about this for every meal for his whole life. There are also lots of different everyday foods that he can't have, such as pasta and bread. As well as the limited amount of protein he can eat, he needs to have a special type of protein shake 3 times a day. However, they are not like the protein shakes that you might have after a gym session, which have lots of nice, different flavours. These shakes, which I wanted to try when I was younger despite Cal insisting how bad they are, really do taste like death. Luckily, I have a small flavour sachet which almost makes them bearable, but even with these flavour sachets, they still taste horrible.

Throughout the day, I would like to keep track of the amount that he had so that I could help him meet his target each day. Over time, I got very good at remembering the amount of protein that was in each item of food.

There is a company that would provide all this low-protein food for people who have PKU. They provide everything from flour so that he can make his own bread to low-protein pot noodles to biscuits, which, I might add, are very tasty, and I preferred them to the biscuits that my family used to get. I spoke to my mum recently, who told me the story of how the first time Cal came over to our house as kids, he came with a long list of stuff he could and could not have, and how much protein was in each thing. Even though we are now in our late 20s, there is still a section in my parents' larder (small understairs cupboard) with Cal's food in.

This has all meant that he is a very healthy man, who, from a very early age, learned how to cook his own food using a lot of vegetables. This resulted in him becoming a very good cook from an early age. He makes a very good pasta sauce from scratch, only using vegetables and no meat, as it has lots of protein.

On a couple of occasions, he has gone out to eat with friends who didn't know he had PKU, and they have complained that there was nothing for them to eat due to their being vegetarian or vegan. This has always been met with a laugh from him, with an explanation that he would most likely only be able to order a portion of chips or a salad, as this would be the only thing that would meet his protein requirements. There are a few restaurants that have been frequented by us as friends, as they have more options for Cal, and others, like Italian restaurants, we never go to, as there is pretty much nothing he can have.

There was a group of us that used to go rock climbing a couple of times a week and then go for a meal and a pint afterward. The two restaurants that we used to go to were Nando's and Wagamama's. Japanese cuisine uses a lot of vegetables, which gives it lots of options, and the rise of veganism has meant that lots of restaurants have started adding vegan and vegetarian options onto the menu, creating a lot of new places and meals he can eat.

Going back 10 years, it was a lot harder for him to stick to his diet as there weren't many products readily available that met his protein requirements, in the last few year the amount of vegan products has increased massively, which gives him a lot more options when doing his weekly food shop, and he doesn't have to completely rely on the low protein products that are specifically produced for people with PKU.

Versatility

In my opinion, potatoes are one of the most versatile foods on the whole planet. There are so many things that can be done with a potato, and I try and cover a lot of different ones in this chapter.

In different cultures, different foods are more popular. For example, rice is eaten very commonly in Asia, and in Germany, potatoes are one of the most popular foods that are eaten.

You can do so many different things with potatoes and cook them in so many ways. They are normally presented as a side and not the main attraction of the dish.

I personally think that potatoes should be more celebrated than they currently are. I could eat potatoes in various forms most days of the week.

Everyone will have their own favourite form of potato, and I think that you would struggle to find someone who doesn't like any type of potato. Ranging from chips, to mash, to baked and boiled, you can do almost anything with a potato.

Potatoes are also one of the main ingredients in gnocchi, mixed with mashed potatoes, flour, and egg.

Air Fried Chips

This is a no-nonsense way of making great crispy chips that you do not need to boil or pre-cook in any way.

Ingredients:

2 medium-sized potatoes per person.

Method:

- Clean the outside of the potatoes and cut them into thin chip shapes, and place into a bowl of ice water. Wash the potatoes in the bowl to remove as much of the starch as possible.

- Take the chips out of the bowl, dry them off, and place in a large bowl. Add the seasoning of your choice and shake the bowl to cover all the chips evenly.

- Place the chips in the air fryer at 190 °C and set the timer for 30 minutes. Shake every 5-10 minutes so that all sides of the chips cook evenly.

Pomme Anna

This is a delicate French dish, which is very straightforward and looks a lot more complicated than it is, and tastes much better than the sum of its parts. It works perfectly as a side to accompany a main such as steak or chicken. This recipe will require an oven safe frying pan, if you do not have one of these then there is a second method underneath. This will be easier if this frying pan has a lid.

Ingredients:

- 1kg potatoes – for 4 people
- Butter
- Salt and black pepper

Method:

- Preheat the oven to 180 ºC.
- Wash and peel the potatoes, and then slice the potatoes as thin as you can; the easiest way to do this is with a mandolin if you have one.
- Put an oven-safe frying pan on medium-low heat and add a tsp of butter and let it melt. Lay the slices of potato in the frying pan so that they are just overlapping to ensure that there are no gaps.
- Once the first layer is complete, add salt, black pepper, and 2 tsp of butter, and then add another layer of potatoes on top with more butter, salt, and pepper.
- Repeat this process layer by layer until all the potatoes are used up.
- Cover the potatoes with a sheet of baking paper and place in the oven to finish cooking for 20-25 minutes.
- You will know when the potatoes are cooked as they will be nice and soft.
- Take the frying pan out of the oven, remove the baking paper, and put a plate large enough to cover the frying pan over the top and flip it over so the dish is on the plate. You should be able to lift the frying pan off, leaving the potatoes on the plate. The top layer of potatoes should be nice and caramelised.
- I found the best way to serve this is to cut it into slices like a pizza.
- If you do not have an oven safe frying pan, then once all the layers of potato have been put in the frying pan. Turn the heat all the way down and put the lid on the frying pan and cook until the potatoes on the top are nice and soft. It is very easy with this method to burn the bottom. If you do don't worry it will still taste very nice.

Creamy Mash Potato

FEEDS 4 AS A SIDE DISH

Whether it is a side to complement the main dish or whether it is the star of the show, mash potato is a great option for the cold and dark winter evenings or as an alternative to roast potatoes alongside a Sunday roast throughout the year.

Ingredients:

- 600g peeled potatoes (150g pp)
- 200g butter
- 50ml of cream
- A sprinkle of salt
- A sprinkle of pepper
- 2 cups of grated cheese of your choice—my personal favourite is extra mature cheddar or Brei. If using Brei, reduce the amount by half as it is quite a strong flavour (optional)
- Sprig of parsley to garnish (optional)

Method:

- Bring a large pot of water to a rolling boil. Peel and chop the potatoes into quarters for faster cooking. Once the water has started boiling, put the potatoes in the water and set a timer for 20 minutes.
- Once a knife can pass easily through the potatoes, they are ready to mash. Strain the potatoes and press them through a potato ricer into a large bowl or back into the same pot used to boil them. If you do not have a potato ricer, then you can push them through a sieve to achieve a similar consistency. It is harder and does take longer.
- Once all the potatoes have been mashed, cube up the butter and add to the potatoes and mix well until the butter is completely incorporated into the mash.
- Add the cream and stir well until incorporated. At this point, you can additionally add the grated cheese and, once again, stir until there are no lumps of cheese and it is smooth.

Curried Bombay Potatoes

This is a great little dish to have as a side, which will add a little bit of spice to the meal. The heat level can be altered for the eater's preference. I like to serve this alongside some fish, such as cod, and steamed veg.

Ingredients:

- 750g potatoes
- 1 jar of sun-dried tomatoes in oil, 280g-168g of tomatoes
- 2tsp of ground turmeric
- 2cm finely diced ginger
- 2tsp curry powder (I use mild)
- 400ml vegetable stock
- 4 cloves of minced garlic
- 1 onion diced

Method:

- Cube up the potatoes into bite-sized pieces and boil them for 10-15 minutes or until they are cooked. Strain them and place them to one side.
- In a large frying pan, add in the diced onion and ginger on medium heat for 7-10 minutes until fragrant.
- Finely dice the sundried tomatoes and add them into the frying pan with the minced garlic and stir well and cook for another 10 minutes.
- Add in the ground turmeric and curry powder and mix these in well.
- Add in the potatoes and stir well so that it is fully incorporated.
- Top with the vegetable stock, turn the heat down to low, and let it cook until all the liquid has been absorbed into the potatoes.

Crispy Parmesan Potatoes

Crispy parmesan potatoes make a great side that puts a little twist on the classic side of boiled new potatoes.

Ingredients:

- 4 small new potatoes per person
- Grated Parmesan
- Paprika
- Mixed herbs
- Salt and black pepper

Method:

- Preheat the oven to 200 ºC.
- Put a saucepan of water onto boil and season well with salt.
- Once the water is boiling, put in the new potatoes and boil for 10-15 minutes; this will depend on the size of the potatoes.
- Once you can pierce the potatoes easily with a sharp knife, strain them and place them to one side.
- Line a baking tray with a sheet of baking paper and, using the small side of the grater, grate a small pile of Parmesan, spaced evenly on it.
- Place a potato on each pile of cheese and push down using a flat surface like the bottom of a glass until it's breaking at the sides and around 1cm thick.
- Season the top of each smashed potato with a sprinkle of paprika, mixed herbs, and black pepper.
- Place the tray in the oven and cook until the Parmesan has become crispy, this should take between 10 and 20 minutes.

Potato Wedges

These are very similar to the chips that I also have in the chapter, but in a different form. I cook them using an air fryer; they can also be cooked using an oven, but I find it best to get the outside nice and crispy and the inside nice and fluffy.

Ingredients:

1-2 potatoes per person, depending on appetite
- 1tsp garlic powder
- 1tsp paprika

Method:

- Cut the potatoes in half, lengthwise, and then into halves again. Depending on the size of the potatoes, cut them into skinnier wedge sizes.
- Toss the wedges in a large bowl with the garlic powder and paprika.
- Place in the air fryer with the ridge facing up.
- Spray the top of the wedges with fry light and air fry for 30 minutes at 180 °C or until the outside is golden brown and the interior is nice and fluffy.

My Dauphinoise Potatoes

This is my take on dauphinoise potatoes with a slight twist to it. This is a great side dish, and I find it works well with a protein, such as chicken or fish, and some steamed veg.

Ingredients:

- 4 large potatoes
- 1 tbsp
- 5 cloves of garlic
- 3tbsp butter
- 1 tsp English mustard
- 1 white onion
- 600ml single cream
- 10g grated parmesan
- Salt and black pepper

Method:

- Pre-heat the oven to 200 C
- Peel the potatoes and using a mandolin slice the potatoes nice and thin.
- Dice the onion and put in a medium heat frying pan with the butter and cook for 5 minutes until they start soften, add in the garlic and cook for an additional 5 minutes.
- Turn the heat down to low and add in the cream, parmesan, paprika and mustard.
- Stir until all mixed together.
- Add the sliced potato into the cream so that it is all evenly coated.
- Layer the potatoes in an oven dish and place in the oven and cook for 30 minutes. After 30 minutes, take the tin foil off, turn the oven down to 180 degrees, and cook for a further 20 minutes.

Roast Potatoes and Carrots

These are always two must-haves for me when having a roast dinner. The easiest way I find to cook these is alongside the chicken in the roast, so that you get the flavour from the chicken in the potatoes.

Ingredients:

- 2 potatoes per person (depending on appetite)
- 2 carrots per person (depending on appetite)
- 2tbsp butter
- 3tbsp oil

Method:

- Preheat the oven to 180 ºC.
- Cut the potatoes into quarters or, if they are a bit bigger, just into bite-sized chunks.
- Cut the carrots into batons.
- Place the butter and oil in a roasting tin and spread out the potatoes and carrots so that they are not overlapping.
- Place in the oven for 45 minutes or 1 hour.
- Give them a stir around halfway through.
- If you are cooking them with a chicken or another roast, which takes around an hour, place them around the outside of the meat and roast for 30 minutes, which will give the flavour from the meat to fuse into the potatoes and carrots.
- After 30 minutes, transfer the meat to a different tray and continue cooking for another 30 minutes until done.

Slow Cooking

Easy Cooking

In my opinion, slow cooking is a very easy and great way to cook different meals when you don't have a lot of time and need something ready for the evening. When I am working during the day, I prep the meal in the morning before I go to work, and then it is done/almost done when I get home from work.

It is also a great way to get the most out of some tougher cuts of meat and get them to taste amazing. Braising beef is a great example of this; it is usually from the shoulder of the cow, which is the most used muscle of the cow, making it one of the toughest. Slow cooking is a great way to break down the connective tissue and make the meat nice and tender.

You can cook so many different meals in a slow cooker, and it is a great way to save time if you are a busy person and don't have a lot of time when you get back from work, but still want a delicious meal to come home to.

Cooking food in a slow cooker normally breaks the meat apart, as cooking it low and slow will dissolve the connective tissue between the muscles in the meat. If you want to keep the meat whole, it might not always be the most appropriate way of cooking.

The most popular thing cooked in the slow cooker in my house is the pulled pork I have listed in this chapter. It is very versatile and can be used for lots of different recipes. It normally goes on top of chips to make dirty fries.

Slow cooker recipes can be very simple or can be more completed with more ingredients. If you take the pulled pork as an example and just put pork and water into a slow cooker for 8 hours on low, you will still get tasty pulled pork. Adding more ingredients, however, gives more layers to the flavour and adds more complexity to the flavour for a richer and tastier dish.

Slow Cook Beef Stew

FEEDS 5 AS A MAIN WITH A SIDE

This is an ideal meal for when you do not have a lot of time in the evening, and can be prepped either in the morning or even the night before. I find that it pairs very well with the mash potato recipe earlier in the book, especially in the winter when the evenings are dark and cold, and you need something to warm you up.

Ingredients:

- 800g diced beef
- 3 large carrots
- 4 sticks of celery
- 2 tbsp tomato puree
- 1 tsp dried oregano
- 1 tsp dried thyme
- 1 tsp dried rosemary
- 3 minced cloves of garlic
- 1 diced white onion
- 500ml red wine
- 250ml water
- 2 beef stock cubes
- 2 tsp corn flour

Method:

- Place the diced beef in a frying pan on high heat with a dash of oil and brown the beef on all sides.
- Remove the beef and add it into the slow cooker.
- Add the diced onion into the frying pan and cook for 5 minutes until it starts to soften.
- Add minced garlic and cook for an additional 2-4 minutes.
- Slice the celery and add this into the frying pan as well. Cook for 10 – 15 minutes on low until it starts to soften.
- Add tomato puree and cook until the smell of raw tomato dissipates.
- Add red wine and stir until it is all combined.
- Add in the oregano, rosemary and thyme.
- Transfer the contents of the frying pan into the slow cooker.
- Add the stock cubes and water and mix through.
- Mix the corn flour with a splash of water into a slurry and add this into the mixture. This will help the sauce thicken.
- Put the slow cooker on low and cook for at least 6 hours. You can cook this for a lot longer if needed.
-

Pulled Pork

Pulled pork can be incredibly easy to make and always seems harder than it is. It can also be used in lots of different recipes.

Ingredients:

- 4 pork shoulder steaks or 700g pork shoulder
- 3tbsp tomato ketchup
- 250ml apple juice
- 250ml vegetable stock
- 3tbsp barbecue sauce
- 3tbsp dark sugar

Method:

- Put the pork shoulder, tomato ketchup, apple juice, vegetable stock, and dark sugar into the slow cooker and put on low for 6-10 hours. The meat will be finished at 6 hours, but I always put it on before I go to work, so it's normally on for around 8-9 hours.
- After 6 hours or so, you will be able to shred the meat. Once the meat is shredded, put it back in the liquid to carry on absorbing the flavour if you have the time.
- Once the time has finished, take the pulled pork out and mix it with the BBQ sauce.
- Transfer the juices into a saucepan on low heat and reduce until it thickens to your preferred thickness.
- Use this sauce to pour over the pulled pork just before eating.

Dirty Fries

SERVES 4 WITH EXTRAS

This recipe is usually a go-to when I am out to eat, and so I tried to replicate my favourite one at home, and both my wife and I think that I did a pretty good job.

Ingredients:

- 4 pork shoulder steaks or 700g pork shoulder
- 3tbsp tomato ketchup
- 250ml apple juice
- 250ml vegetable stock
- 3tbsp barbecue sauce
- 3tbsp dark sugar
- 700g frozen chips (skinny skin-on fries are our favourite)
- Grated cheddar (amount depends on how much you like cheese and the size of the dish being used)
- 1 spring onion (optional)
- 1 diced jalapeno (optional)

Method:

- Put the pork shoulder, tomato ketchup, apple juice, vegetable stock, and dark sugar into the slow cooker and put on low for 6-10 hours. The meat will be finished at 6 hours, but I always put it on before I go to work, so it's normally on for around 8-9 hours.
- Once the pork is cooked, take it out. Place it in a bowl and shred it.
- Pour the juices into a saucepan and put on a low heat to start reducing them.
- Start cooking the chips in the air fryer or oven until they start to go crispy, which usually takes around 30-40 minutes.
- Once the chips are cooked, place them in a baking dish and top with the pulled pork and grated cheese. The cheese should go over the top of the pork.
- Bake for 10-20 minutes until the cheese has melted.
- Top with the sliced spring onion and jalapeno.
- The juice from the slow cooker should have reduced into a thick gravy-like sauce. Pour this over the top of the completed dish and serve.

Cheesy Shredded Chicken Burger

These are very easy to make and very tasty

Ingredients:

- 1 chicken breast per person
- 100ml chicken stock per person
- 1 burger bun per person
- Grated mozzarella (amount depends on how cheesy you like it for yourself. 1 ball of mozzarella will do two people)
- Grated cheddar (same amount as the mozzarella)
- BBQ sauce
- Black beans - 100g per person (optional)
- Coleslaw (optional)

Method:

- Put the chicken and chicken stock in the slow cooker and cook on low for 4-8 hours or high for 3-5 hours, depending on how much time you have. I normally put it on low when I leave for work in the morning.
- When the chicken has 1 hour left, shred the chicken and add in the strained beans if you are going to use them.
- Once the chicken has fully cooked, add in the mozzarella, cheddar, and BBQ sauce.
- Mix it all in together until the cheese has melted, and it is evenly distributed.
- Place the mixture on a lightly toasted burger bun.
- Serve alongside chips or sweet potato fries.

Desserts

Sweet Tooth

As long as I can remember, I have had a massive sweet tooth and have always loved sweet things. When I was young, I used to take a big chunk of marzipan, and I used to hide it underneath my parents' dining room table, tucked away in the corner. When I was able to and no one was looking, I would sneak under the table and have a little nibble to satisfy my craving.

Most of my family also has a sweet tooth just as bad as mine. Every year, my mum puts on an Easter egg hunt on Easter Sunday around the garden at her house for my family to find. Every single year, an extortionate amount of chocolate gets eaten.

At my grandparents' house, they have a drawer in their kitchen full of sweets and chocolate, which gets very frequently topped up as my grandad has the biggest sweet tooth of all of us. When I was growing up, he would always have different flavours of ice cream for dessert when we went out to eat.

The ice cream van used to stop outside their house as the driver knew that as soon as he played the tune, my grandad would come out with his special ice cream bowl and spoon and get 3 scoops.

When we went over to their house in the summer when my sister and I were kids, we would go straight to the sweet drawer and raid it for the treasures inside. My grandma would always make sure that it was full for when we came to visit.

My love of sweet things carried on into adulthood, and before I started my diet, my mother-in-law, one year, got me a 1.5kg tub of Biscoff spread and 300 Biscoff biscuits for Christmas. I would get one biscuit and use it to scoop up some of the spread and sandwich it with the other side of the biscuit. Embarrassingly, it did not take me too long to get through the entire tub and all the biscuits.

Kaiserschmarrn

Kaiserschmarrn is a Bavarian dessert that is very similar to pancakes but thicker and torn into pieces. It is traditionally served with a side of apple sauce or hot jam. It is something that I always try to have when I go back to Germany and replicate as often as my diet will allow me back home.

Ingredients:

- 4 eggs
- 120g flour
- 250ml milk
- 3tbsp sugar
- 30ml rum
- 2tbsp icing sugar
- 50g raisins

Method:

- Separate the eggs and put them in two separate bowls.
- In the bowl with the yolks, add the flour, milk, rum, and 1 tbsp sugar and mix well until fully combined.
- Add 2 tbsp of sugar and a pinch of salt to the egg whites and mix until you get stiff peaks.
- Fold the fluffy egg whites into the first mixture, one spoon at a time, until fully combined and smooth. Then stir in the raisins.
- Put a knob of butter into a large frying pan on low heat until melted, and then add in the mixture and cover with the lid.
- After 5 – 10 minutes, the mixture should start to firm up. Flip it over; this is made a lot easier by cutting it into 4 pieces. If you smell that it is starting to burn sooner, then flip it over.
- Let the other side cook for a couple of minutes, and then rip it up into small pieces while still in the pan.
- Once the whole this is completely ripped, sprinkle over 1 tbsp icing sugar and stir until it has dissolved
- Plate it up and then dust over 1 tbsp icing sugar to finish it off.

Granny Tash's Pavlova

This is a staple of all of our family get-togethers and is always the first to be polished off.

Ingredients:

- 4 egg whites
- 220g of caster sugar
- 1tbsp of white wine vinegar
- 1tbsp of cornflour
- 300ml whipping cream
- Some seasonal fruit

Method:

- Preheat the oven to 180 degrees.
- Separate the egg whites from the yolks and put the egg whites in a large mixing bowl. Mix the egg whites on high speed until you get stiff peaks. On medium speed, slowly mix in two tablespoons of sugar at a time, mixing it in each time, making sure that the sugar is fully incorporated each time.
- Once all the sugar is fully incorporated, add the tablespoon of white wine vinegar and mix it in on low speed. Once fully incorporated, mix in the tablespoon of cornflour again on low speed. Once this is fully incorporated, the mixture should look glossy.
- On a flat baking tray, place a sheet of baking paper. It helps to stick it down with a small dab of the mixture.
- Spoon the mixture onto the baking tray in a circle in a shallow well so that the toppings will fit nicely into it.
- Before putting the mixture in the oven, turn it down to 140 degrees and set the timer for 35 minutes.
- It is ready when it looks like the picture on the outside, and when you lightly press down, you can feel it is still lightly spongy underneath.
- Once it is completely cooled, then whip the 300ml of whipping cream and spoon it onto the centre of the pavlova and spread it out evenly, and then top with your chosen fruit. Our go-to are raspberries and strawberries.

Oma's Biscoff Cheesecake

This is one of the favourite things that my mother has ever made. It is very rich and extremely delicious and perfect for a bring-and-share or a birthday cake (I have had it as a birthday cake on multiple occasions).

Ingredients:

- 250g crushed Biscoff biscuits
- 100g melted unsalted butter
- 225ml double cream
- 125g caster sugar
- 675g cream cheese
- 2 tsp vanilla extract
- 300g melted smooth Biscoff spread
- 100g melted milk chocolate
- 100g melted white chocolate

Make the base:

- Whizz the biscuits to a fine crumb in a food processor, then add the melted butter and mix well. Pour this mixture into the bottom of a lined springform tin, pressing well to make sure it is even on all sides. Set the base to one side.
- Whisk the cream until stiff peaks form, and set this to one side.
- In a separate bowl, beat together caster sugar, cream cheese, and vanilla extract. Mix until it is smooth and consistent. Add the whipped cream by gently folding it through with a spatula.
- Separate this mixture evenly into 3 bowls. To the first bowl, add 100g of the melted Biscoff spread. To the second one, the melted milk chocolate, and to the third one, the melted white chocolate.
- Pour the milk chocolate mixture onto the base, spread evenly, then pour the Biscoff mixture on top, spread evenly, and lastly, pour the white chocolate mixture.
- Let the cake sit for a minimum of 3 hours.
- Melt the remaining 200g of Biscoff spread (the best way to do this evenly, I found, is with a Bain-Marie), and very gently pour over the set cake.
- Let it sit in the fridge until the Biscoff spread on top is completely cool and set.

Sweet Apple Parcels

This is a sweet alternative to the savoury option that I had earlier in the book.

Ingredients:

- 200g self-raising flour
- 150g Greek yogurt
- 3 tbsp soft brown sugar
- 3 tsp white sugar
- 1 finely diced large apple
- 10 berries (in this, I have used quartered strawberries, but most other berries would also work)
- 1 tsp cinnamon
- 100ml single cream

Method:

- Put the apple, white sugar, and cinnamon into a saucepan on low heat and stir every 30 seconds or so to ensure that the sugar does not burn or stick to the bottom of the pan.
- In a large mixing bowl, add the flour, Greek yogurt, and soft brown sugar and mix well to combine.
- Turn the dough out onto a lightly floured work surface and knead until you get a smooth dough.
- Separate the dough into 4 even pieces and roll out flat using a rolling pin. The dough should be thin but not yet see-through.
- Once the apple has softened to your preferred texture, add in your berries and stir.
- Place a tbsp of the apple mixture into the centre of each circle of dough.
- Bring 2 opposite sides together in the middle and then crimp your way around, sealing it as you go.
- Push down on the top once sealed so that it is around 1cm thick.
- Place in a dry frying pan on very low heat.
- Flip over every 2-3 minutes to make sure that it is cooking evenly.
- Once both sides are golden brown, place on a plate and drizzle over the single cream.

Chocolate Parcels

This is a very similar recipe to the sweet apple parcels, but for the chocolate lovers.

Ingredients:

- 200g self-raising flour
- 150g Greek yogurt
- 3 tbsp demerara sugar
- 2 tbsp cocoa powder
- 3 Kinder chocolate bars per parcel
- 1 tsp chocolate spread per parcel
- Around 10 mini marshmallows

Method:

- In a large mixing bowl, add the flour, Greek yogurt, demerara sugar, and cocoa powder and mix well to combine.
- Turn the dough out onto a lightly floured work surface and knead until you get a smooth dough.
- Separate the dough into 4 even pieces and roll out flat using a rolling pin. The dough should be thin but not yet see-through.
- Break the chocolate into squares and place in the centre of the circle with a tsp of chocolate spread on top with the mini marshmallows.
- Bring two opposite sides together in the middle and then crimp your way around, sealing it as you go.
- Push down on the top once sealed so that it is around 1cm thick.
- Place in a dry frying pan on very low heat.
- Flip over every 2-3 minutes to make sure that it is cooking evenly.
- Once both sides are golden brown, place on a plate and drizzle over the single cream.

Banana Cookies

This is one of my wife's favourite types of cookies to make at home. I got the idea from another cookbook that she has. But when she asked me to make them, we didn't have all the right ingredients, so I improvised and changed it a bit. She said that they were very nice, different from her regular ones, but very nice all the same, and personally, I prefer them. They are very quick and easy to do and are a great little snack.

Ingredients:

- 2 very ripe bananas
- 200g plain flour
- 2 tsp vanilla extract
- 60g brown demerara sugar
- 60g melted butter
- 1 tsp bicarbonate of soda

Method:

- Preheat the oven to 180 degrees.
- Mix all the ingredients in a large mixing bowl until they form a smooth batter.
- Spoon out even-sized pieces onto a baking tray covered with baking paper.
- Cook for 12-15 minutes until they are starting to go brown, but they are still soft to the touch.
- Take them out of the oven and let them cool on the side.

Oma s Rainbow Jelly

This was a staple of every single childhood birthday that my sister or I had, and everyone always enjoyed it. This does take a few days to do due to the setting time, so it needs to be planned in advance.

Ingredients:

- An assortment of different flavours of make-your-own jelly

Method:

- Melt the first flavour of jelly and pour into a large mixing/serving bowl. Set it aside in the fridge and wait for it to set. Make sure to use half the amount of water that the packet says. For example, the jelly I normally use says to mix the concentrated jelly with 300ml of boiling water and then 300ml of cold water once it has dissolved. For this recipe, you need to just add the 300ml of boiling water so that it is more concentrated. This will intensify and create a stronger colour and, therefore, a stronger contrast between colours.

- Once the first layer has set, melt down the second flavour and pour very carefully on top of the first layer, making sure not to break through the first layer so that you get clear lines.

- Repeat this process with all the flavours until the bowl is full of different colours/flavours of jelly.

German Chocolate Cake

This is a rich, fudgy chocolate cake that is great for the chocolate lovers out there. Fun fact, this style of chocolate cake was invented by an English American man called Samual German and did not originate in the country of Germany.

Ingredients:

For the cake

- 400g granulated sugar
- 210g plain flour
- 75g cocoa powder
- 1 ½ tsp baking powder
- 1 ½ tsp bicarbonate of soda
- 1 tsp salt
- 2 eggs
- 240ml buttermilk
- 120ml vegetable oil
- 2 tsp vanilla extract
- 240ml boiling water

For the frosting

- 115g soft butter
- 65g cocoa powder
- 400g icing sugar
- 90ml evaporated milk
- 1 tsp vanilla extract
- 15ml Amaretto

Method:

- Preheat oven to 190 ºC.
- In a large mixing bowl, combine the sugar, flour, cocoa powder, baking powder, bicarbonate of soda, and salt.
- Once combined, mix in the eggs, buttermilk, oil and vanilla extract. Mix all these ingredients together until they form a smooth batter, and then mix in the boiling water. (The batter will be very runny but that is okay.)
- Pour the batter into 2 8-9-inch greased cake tins, and bake for 30-35 minutes.
- Once cooked, take them out of the oven and let them cool completely.
- While the cakes are cooling, make the frosting by using an electric whisk to cream 115g soft butter and then add the cocoa powder and icing sugar. Add the Amaretto and vanilla extract, and then the evaporated milk, a little bit at a time, until you get a smooth frosting.
- Put half the frosting on top of the bottom cake, put the second one on top, and then decorate the top of the second cake with the leftover frosting.
- Make sure you leave enough to pipe on top.

Great Gran's Victoria Sponge

This is a staple of any family get-together, or even just a visit for a chat and a cup of tea.

Ingredients:

- 170g white sugar
- 170g self-raising flour
- 170g soft butter
- 3 large eggs
- 1 tsp baking powder
- 1 tsp vanilla extract
- 1 tbsp icing sugar
- 300ml whipping cream
- Chopped strawberries

Method:

- Preheat oven to 180 °C.
- In a large bowl, mix together the flour, sugar, eggs, butter, baking powder, and vanilla extract.
- Grease 2 8-inch baking trays, and split the batter evenly between the two trays.
- Place in the oven and bake for 22 minutes.
- Take the cakes out of the trays and let them cool on a wire rack.
- While the cakes are cooling, you can make the filling.
- Whisk the cream in a bowl and then add chopped strawberries and mix well.
- Once the cakes are cool, cut the top off one of them so that it is nice and flat. Use this cake as the base.
- Put the cream on top of the bottom cake.
- Put the second cake on top and put a thin dusting of icing sugar on top of that.

Snack Bars

These are a great little bar which can be added into lunch boxes or are great for weekends.

Ingredients:

- 320g oats
- 130g peanut butter
- 115g honey
- 25g chocolate chips

Method:

- Mix all the ingredients, except the optional chocolate together in a large flat tray and press down to make sure it is flat and level.
- If you are adding the decorative chocolate, put a layer of milk chocolate over the whole thing and then drizzle the white chocolate in lines across. To feather the chocolate, use a toothpick to draw a line across the white chocolate lines.
- Place in the fridge ideally overnight, but if you don't have that much time, just until it is solid.
- Cut into the size of bars and enjoy.

Mango Sorbet

I have always wanted to get a ice cream maker but have never been able to justify the expense when it will most likely be used a few times in the summer and then be put away in a cupboard for 9 months. This is a very basic recipe that only requires a food processor and is healthier than regular ice cream.

Ingredients:

- 500g frozen mango chunks
- 4 tbsp Greek yogurt
- 1 tbsp honey

Method:

- Put the frozen mango into the food processor put it on low for around 1 minute. The chunks should now be around the same size as rice.
- Add in the Greek yogurt and honey.
- Mix until the mixture has a smooth and creamy texture.

Baby Food Ideas

Discovery

My wife and I have discovered that having your first child in the 2020s means that you're googling what you need to do all the time, especially when it came to food and figuring out when we should start weaning Otto off breastmilk and onto solid food. Some of the products that you can buy say that they are suitable for babies from 4 months old. Having done other research and spoken to family members, basically everything else said from around 6 months old. However, we found that Otto was showing a big interest in food from around 5 months old. A lot of people had told us that he would show us when he was ready to start eating solid foods. At 5 months old, he was reaching for our food and staring at us while we were eating. We took this as him telling us that he was ready to start trying solid foods.

My wife has been brilliant in doing all her research to know what we should be doing and when we should start doing it with him. She read that it was important for Otto to watch us eat as soon as he could. As soon as he could be put in his bouncer, we would put him in it on the table, and he would watch us eat. He started showing us that he was ready to eat solid foods at around 5 months old, but being new parents, we were really worried about starting too soon, as most of our research said we should start at 6 months.

We finally caved at 5 and a half months and started him on some pureed carrot. It is safe to say that he was not sure about the texture of it, as this was the first thing that he had eaten that wasn't breastmilk. He wasn't sure what to do, so he spent most of the time trying to gum the rim of the bowl. Over the next week or so, we explored different foods with different textures.

My wife went on a course about baby nutrition and different ways to wean babies. She learned that there were two main types. The first was adult-led weaning, which is where the parent feeds the baby with a spoon. The second is baby-led weaning, which is where you put different foods in front of the baby and let them pick them up and try them out. Safe to say that this led to quite a big mess and lots of food has been thrown on the floor. Luckily, we have 2 labradors who make sure it gets cleaned up incredibly quickly.

Most of the food in this section is aimed at babies who are around 9 months and older, as before that point, most babies will just have pureed/whole foods, such as strawberries. All babies are different, and some may need more time, and some may be able to have different foods sooner. Some of the chewier ones, such as the snack bars, may need teeth to get through. As he gets older, he is eating increasingly more food. Now at 9 months old he is now on 3 meals a day and is learning how to eat without it going all over his face. This does not mean sadly that we are in a mess-free house as the food that doesn't end up on his face usually ends up on the floor instead. This makes the dogs incredibly happy, as they are our live vacuums.

He is starting to develop likes and dislikes which seem to change quite frequently, just as we are leaning what he seems to like then these changes and the next time we give him that food, most of it ends up on the floor. One thing that seems to be an ever present in his likes list is different types of fruit. On top of this list is bananas. He will very happily eat half a banana in one go.

On our recent holiday to France, it seemed unfair to not let him try a bit of croissant for the first time, it's safe to say that he very much enjoyed it.

Broccoli Bake

Ingredients:

- 80g steamed broccoli
- 3 eggs
- 50g finely grated carrots
- 20g grated mild cheddar

Method:

- Preheat oven to 180 ºC.
- Steam the broccoli for 15-20 minutes until very soft.
- Once cooked, put them in a baking dish and mash using a fork.
- Add in the grated carrot, cheese, and 3 eggs.
- Mix all the ingredients together until thoroughly combined.
- Place in the oven and bake for 20-25 minutes.
- Take out of the oven and let cool before cutting into snack-size pieces.

Sweet Potato Puree

Ingredients:
- 1 sweet potato
- 30g cooked mince meat
- 1 tsp oil

Method:
- Cook the sweet potato by either baking it in the oven for 45-60 minutes at 190 °C, depending on the size of the potato. Or you can peel it and then boil it until you can cut through it easily with a knife. This should take around 20 minutes.
- While this is cooking, fry off the mincemeat but without any seasonings.
- Once they are both cooked, put the sweet potato in a bowl and mash.
- Once mashed, add in the mince and oil and mix until fully combined.

Broccoli Avocado Pasta

Ingredients:

- 100g Broccoli
- Half an avocado
- 4 tbsp Greek yogurt
- 90g dried pasta

Method:

- Start boiling a pot of water and cook the pasta for 10-12 minutes or until done.
- Boil the broccoli
- Add the boiled broccoli, avocado and Greek yogurt to a food processor and blend until smooth.
- Once the pasta is cooked, strain it and mix in the sauce.

Oat Bars

Ingredients:

- 3 ripe bananas
- 350g oats
- 4 tbsp coconut oil

Method:

- Preheat the oven to 180 ºC.
- Mash the bananas in a bowl and then add in the oats.
- Add in the coconut oil and mix to fully combine.
- Place the mixture on a baking tray lined with baking paper.
- Place another piece of baking paper on top and, using a rolling pin, roll the mixture flat until it is around 1cm thick.
- Take the top piece of baking paper off. Put it in the oven and cook for 15 - 20 minutes.
- Once cooked, take it out of the oven and let it cool.
- Once cool, cover the top with the melted chocolate and cut into bar-sized pieces.

Crockets

Ingredients:

- 2 boiled potatoes, peeled
- 80g boiled broccoli
- 40g grated cheese

Method:

- Put a pot of water on the boil.
- Once boiling, cut the potatoes into quarters and put them in the water. Place a colander on top of the pot, put the broccoli in it, and place a lid on the top. The potatoes will boil at the same time as the broccoli will steam.
- Boil/steam for 20 minutes or until very soft.
- Once cooked, transfer both the potatoes and the broccoli into a bowl and mash them smooth.
- Add in the grated cheese and mix until fully combined.
- Form into crocket size, around 2cm long and 1cm wide.
- You can either bake at 180 °C for 25 minutes,

  or

- Put in the air fryer at 180 °C for 20 minutes, flipping halfway through.

Fritters

Ingredients:

- 2 boiled potatoes
- 1 peeled carrot, finely grated
- ½ red pepper finely diced
- 2 tbsp plain flour

Method:

- Peel and cut the potatoes into quarters. Put them in a pot of boiling water and cook for 20 minutes until soft.
- While the potatoes are cooking, peel and grate one carrot and finely dice ½ a red pepper.
- Once the potatoes are done, mash them in a bowl and then add the carrot, pepper, and plain flour.
- Thoroughly mix and form into small round fritters.
- Place in a frying pan with a splash of oil and fry for 5-7 minutes on either side until golden brown.

Chicken and Broccoli Nuggets

Ingredients:

- 80g broccoli, steamed or boiled
- 150g chicken mince
- 20g grated cheese
- 1 egg
- 30g breadcrumbs

Method:

- Pre-heat the oven to 180ºC
- Boil/steam the broccoli for 20 minutes until soft.
- Once cooked, place in a bowl and mash.
- Add in the chicken mince, grated cheese, and egg and mix well until combined.
- Finally, add in the breadcrumbs and mix again until fully incorporated.
- Shape into nugget-size pieces and place in the oven for 15 - 25 minutes. Make sure the chicken is cooked all the way through.

Potato and Pea Bites

Ingredients:

- 250g peeled and boiled potatoes
- 100g peas
- 40g grated cheese
- 2 tbsp breadcrumbs

Method:

- Preheat oven to 180 °C.
- Peel and cut the potatoes into quarters and boil them for 20 minutes or until very soft.
- Put the peas in with the potatoes after around 10 minutes.
- Once cooked, place both in a bowl and mash them up.
- Add in the grated cheese and breadcrumbs and mix well until combined.
- Form into small crocket size pieces, place on a baking tray, and cook for 20-25 minutes until golden brown.

Strawberry and Banana Pancakes

Ingredients:

- 1 ripe banana
- 2 large strawberries
- 1 egg
- 2 tbsp self-raising flour

Method:

- In a large bowl, mash the banana and strawberries until pureed.
- Add in the egg and flour and mix to make the batter.
- In a frying pan, spoon in the mixture into small pancake-sized portions.
- Fry both sides until golden brown and cooked through.

Spinach and Tomato Muffins

Ingredients:

- 2 eggs
- 150g self-raising flour
- 100ml milk
- 1 tbsp olive oil
- 100g grated cheese
- 80g baby spinach
- 5 cherry tomatoes

Method:

- Preheat the oven to 200 ºC.
- Wilt the spinach and squeeze out any excess liquid
- Puree the spinach along with the tomatoes.
- In a large bowl, mix together the eggs, milk, and oil and make sure it is all combined.
- Once it is all combined, add in the flour and mix again.
- Mix in the cheese.
- Add in the spinach and tomato mixture and stir well to make sure it is evenly distributed.
- Grease the muffin tin either with spray or butter and add the mixture into the tins.
- Bake in the oven for 20-25 minutes until they are golden brown.

Sweet Potato Pizza

Ingredients:

- 1 peeled sweet potato
- 50g – 100g plain flour
- 1 tsp Tomato puree per pizza
- Grated cheese

Method:

- Preheat the oven to 200 ºC.
- Peel the sweet potato and boil for 15 – 20 minutes until very soft
- Mash the sweet potato and add in the flour.
- Knead the flour into the sweet potato mash until it has stopped being sticky.
- Divide the dough into 3 even pieces and roll out until thin.
- Spread the tomato puree on top of each one and top with a bit of grated cheese.
- Put in the oven for 10 – 15 minutes, until the cheese has melted.

About the Author

This is Lukas' first book that he has written, and he wanted to capture himself and his family in the book as well as his recipes.

Lukas lives in a small town in the southwest of England but was born in Germany and has lots of family that live there. In the last few years, he has discovered a love of cooking. Lukas has a large extended family, who are all great cooks, and he wants to preserve the recipes from his family. This book was also written for his young son so that he can learn from a young age how to cook.

Acquisition.com Volumen II

Prospectos de $100M Resumen y cuaderno de trabajo

Cómo conseguir que los desconocidos quieran comprar lo que vendes.

ALEX HORMOZI

Acquisition.com
7710 N FM 620, Building 13C, Suite 100, Austin, Texas 78726.